Grant Lukenbill

Untold Millions
Secret Truths About Marketing to Gay and Lesbian Consumers

*Pre-publication
REVIEWS,
COMMENTARIES,
EVALUATIONS . . .*

"**L**ukenbill's perspective on gay and lesbian consumers is exactly what today's business people need. He has written a long-needed book—one that I recommend."

Rick Cirillo
*National Sales Manager,
Gay & Lesbian Community,
American Airlines*

"*U**ntold Millions* is a primer for reaching the gay and lesbian consumer segment, and corporations intent on profiting from the new millennium's fragmented marketplace should use it! In concise and practical language, Grant Lukenbill demystifies the gay and lesbian market, examines research and the limitations of available data, and outlines methods of building a profitable relationship with the market. Marketing decision makers with vision must read and use *Untold Millions*."

Stephanie Blackwood, MS
*Partner, Spare Parts, Inc.
Marketing and Communications,
New York, NY*

"**F**inally, some sanity has been brought to this subject. Lukenbill focuses on the facts, spells out the issues, and dispels the myths. If you conduct business with gay consumers, you need this book."

Steve Levenberg
Founder, Gay & Lesbian
Consumer & Business Expo

"**T**he second edition of Grant Lukenbill's 1995 landmark *Untold Millions* brings a much-needed update to the file on the evolving gay and lesbian consumer market. Supported by meticulous research and Lukenbill's own savvy analysis, this revised edition should be required reading in every corporate boardroom in America.

To some extent, Lukenbill has made the best of a distinct disadvantage: a general dearth of reliable marketing and consumer information about gay men and lesbians. Spotty at best and inaccurate at worst, such data has contributed to some of the tired and bigoted stereotypes that persist about the gay community. Lukenbill punctures many of these prejudicial myths with a new analysis of the industry's gold standard of data: the 1994 Yankelovich MONITOR's Perspective on Gays and Lesbians. Among other characteristics, the Yankelovich survey shows clearly that gay men and lesbians represent a cohesive marketing segment, have strong brand loyalties to companies that demonstrate concern for gay issues, and make up approximately six percent of the American population.

Aiming primarily at corporate America, *Untold Millions* moves from interpretive overview to hard-nosed practical advice for successful marketing to, and community relations with, gay and lesbian communities. The author provides some very practical roadmaps for improving two-way understanding between gay people and the makers of the products they buy. In fact, the book has great value beyond its consumer marketing focus. Any reader—business oriented or otherwise—will come away with much to ponder about what it's like to be gay in turn-of-the-millennium America."

Steve Bolerjack
Journalist and Public Relations
Consultant; Co-Founder,
Gay & Lesbian Marketing Group,
Hill & Knowlton Public Relations,
New York, NY

Untold Millions
Secret Truths About Marketing to Gay and Lesbian Consumers

HAWORTH Gay & Lesbian Studies
John P. De Cecco, PhD
Editor in Chief

Untold Millions

Secret Truths About Marketing to Gay and Lesbian Consumers

Grant Lukenbill

Harrington Park Press
An Imprint of The Haworth Press, Inc.
New York • London • Oxford

Published by

Harrington Park Press, an imprint of The Haworth Press, Inc., 10 Alice Street, Binghamton, NY 13904-1580

Second edition of *Untold Millions: Positioning Your Business for the Gay and Lesbian Consumer Revolution* by Grant Lukenbill, published by HarperBusiness, a division of HarperCollins Publishers, 1995.

Cover design by Jennifer M. Gaska.

Library of Congress Cataloging-in-Publication Data

Lukenbill, Grant.
    Untold millions : secret truths about marketing to gay and lesbian consumers / Grant Lukenbill.
       p. cm.
    Includes bibliographical references and index.
    ISBN 1-56023-948-4 (alk. paper).
    1. Gay consumers—United States. 2. Lesbian consumers—United States. 3. Marketing—United States. I. Title.
HC110.C6L852 1999
658.8′34′086640973—dc21
                                                      98-47911
                                                        CIP

For my kind and gentle brother, Ralph Lukenbill.
And in dear memory of Gary and Kelvin—I miss you both.

ABOUT THE AUTHOR

Grant Lukenbill is President of GLV Communications in New York City. Formerly with *The Advocate,* he helped with the national launch of *Outweek* in 1990 and later began serving as a consultant to businesses such as AT&T, Bell Atlantic, RCA Records, and American Express about the politics and proven strategies needed to reach gay and lesbian consumers. Mr. Lukenbill now speaks internationally on gay and lesbian marketing issues and is currently organizing the first gay and lesbian consumer lobby in the United States. The author of the forthcoming book *Smart Spending for Gay and Lesbian Consumers: What You Really Need to Know Before You Shop, Buy, or Invest,* Mr. Lukenbill is also the co-founder of the Gay and Lesbian Values Ratings and Research Index (GLV 100), which annually surveys the best 100 companies for gay and lesbian consumers and employees.

CONTENTS

Foreword

In *Untold Millions: Secret Truths About Marketing to Gay and Lesbian Consumers,* Grant Lukenbill has written not only a developmental history of emerging corporate ideology, but he goes further by addressing the inherent conflicts that arise within a movement that justifiably prides itself on being different yet welcomes, albeit warily, the attention now being paid to it by the American business community.

One speaker at the 1998 National Gay and Lesbian Task Force annual *Creating Change* meeting in Pittsburgh proclaimed to thunderous applause that she did not spend over twenty years of activism to be reduced to nothing more than a market niche.

Has the community sold itself out? It does seem, even to the casual observer, that you cannot attend any gay-related gathering without seeing the subtle, and sometimes not so subtle, presence of corporate America. Think about it. From ski events to AIDS fundraisers, from rodeos to annual Pride celebrations, from bowling tournaments to the glitzy GLAAD (Gay and Lesbian Alliance Against Defamation) Media Awards, it seems that much of corporate America suddenly has embraced gay culture.

I have witnessed this change from both the inside and outside. In 1975, one year after joining what was then the Bell System, AT&T became one of the first corporations to include sexual orientation in its non-discrimination policies. During my time there I also enjoyed the privilege of being the co-president of LEAGUE, the Lesbian, Bisexual, Gay, and Transgendered United Employees at AT&T. LEAGUE was the first corporate gay employee organization and owes its existence to the 1987 march on Washington. As workplace activists, LEAGUE's members and leaders, as the leaders of similar organizations will attest, are constantly living a dual personality. Are we good company citizens demanding safety and equality for our people and allies or are we there to serve our community by advocating for our external interests? Do we compromise ourselves when we demonstrate to our marketing and public relations directors that doing business with the gay community is a sound business decision for any company truly interested in shareholder value? Do we sacrifice our integrity when we point out that indeed we are a market niche?

If we accept the invitation to dance with corporate America, then we have to let CEOs and other corporate types know that our community wants to be served at that very same table with the rest of the world. We are tired of eating the leftovers. I personally believe that any company boasting about its all-inclusive employment policies, but failing to support the community where it conducts business, is guilty of corporate hypocrisy of the worst kind.

Grant Lukenbill examines many key issues. Particular attention should be paid to the key role that advertising plays. The lucrative results in the short time since Madison Avenue discovered our community are truly astounding. Modern advertising and direct marketing can make or break any attempt to foster brand loyalty, but we must now begin to ask why these images are not placed in mainstream print and electronic media. If we are good enough for ourselves, why are we not presentable to the rest of the country? The community needs to make sure that when leaving the closet, we do not forget to pack corporate America and take it along with us.

Equally important is Lukenbill's critical review of the so-called rich gay community. Numerous studies, surveys, and opinion polls have been undertaken. Whatever your opinion of the results, they have collectively become a thorn in our community's side. However, the statistics so reasonably uncovered by the Yankelovich MONITOR may go a long way toward correcting the misconceptions advanced by inadequate surveys. Regardless of whose figures you believe, the core truth remains that gay, lesbian, bisexual, and transgendered people deserve respect regardless of economic status, educational level, racial grouping, or gender identification.

Untold Millions will serve as an excellent blueprint for any corporation planning a relationship with us. Gay employee organizations would do well to send copies to their company's leadership. Gay consumers must be vigilant and not assume that because a corporate logo is waving over an event, the company is gay friendly. Our national and local organizations need to be totally honest with corporate sponsors. There will definitely be times when our interests will not be mutually shared. This does not, however, excuse any corporation from investing in our good will, nor should we walk away from the opportunities that continued dialogues present. There is an old Native American prophecy declaring, "A new tribe of people shall come unto the earth from many colors, classes, and creeds. They will be known as the Warriors of the Rainbow." These are the Untold Millions that Grant Lukenbill has so ably written about.

John Klenert
Executive Director
AT&T LEAGUE Foundation

Acknowledgments

This book reflects the contributions and commitments of many people. For listening, strategizing, and conducting historical, groundbreaking research on gay and lesbian Americans as consumers, I am most grateful to the wise and talented people at Yankelovich Partners, Inc.—particularly Rex Briggs for his team spirit, critical thinking, and formulation of the Psychology of Disenfranchisement.

For permission to include some of the most pioneering on-line research of gay and lesbian consumers to date, I am equally indebted to the people at Greenfield Online, Inc., and to their partnership with Stephanie Blackwood and Scott Seitz of Spare Parts, Inc.

Although too numerous to mention individually, I thank all the people at the daily newspapers and gay and lesbian publications across the country who contributed their time, opinions, research, databases and Rolodexes to this work. Numerous individuals at gay- and lesbian-owned small businesses have made important contributions as well, and I am grateful for their time and professional courtesies.

For constructive criticism, mature debate, and encouragement from the beginning, I'm particularly indebted to my friends and trusted confidantes: Adrian Milton, David Winters, and Michael Gast. I also want to acknowledge the contributions and personal support I have received from Dorothy Atcheson, Sidney Casares, Chad Edwards, Amy Ginsberg, Neil Goldman, Jay Hill, David Kraft-Schutte, Nan Liebowitz, Josie Marode, Stan Redfern, David Rephun, Bob Riner, Lois Sheeler, Lisa Tritico, Steve Turtell, Steve Walton, and Jimmy Wilmore. I thank Bill Dobbs for always reminding me of my roots.

My thanks to Frank Mount, Charlotte Sheedy, and Adrian Zackheim for their contributions to this book's first edition. And for editing the early manuscripts and providing patient, competent advice on structure, I am grateful to Virginia Smith, Jane Loeb, and Suzanne Oaks.

For believing in and supporting this book's second edition, I thank Bill Palmer at The Haworth Press, as well as Peg Marr and her associates, who made extensive contributions well above the call of duty.

Thanks to my bibliographer Janet Kvamme, for her keen sense of history—and especially her work in association with James Briggs Murray at the Schomburg Library in Harlem. Extensive thanks are due as well to my trusted friend and art buddy, Patrick Arena, for his patience and loyal editorial and research assistance. And to Ron Niemann, whom I love most for his unswerving commitment to spiritual friendship and a sense of humor too twisted for words but well-appreciated during the burning of midnight oil.

For inspiration and endless reams of newspaper clippings, letters, pictures, phone calls, faxes, e-mail, and a highly balanced sense of what constitutes community, I want to acknowledge the editorial contributions and shrewd—at times ironic—political insights of my brother, Ralph Lukenbill.

Others have contributed priceless gems of insight as well: Dan Baker, Matthew Bank, Amanda Bearse, Allan Bérubé, Stephanie Blackwood, Jay Blotcher, Steve Bolerjack, Howard Buford, Dennis Colby, Bob Craig, Dan Dailey, Rob Davis, John Dellassandro, Michael Denneny, former New York City Mayor David Dinkins, the Honorable Tom Duane, Martin Duberman, Murray Edelman, Stuart Elliott, Paula Ettlebrick, Mildred Gardner, Stephen Gendin, Timothy J. Gilfoyle, Barbara Gittings, Michael Goff, David Gold, Barbara Grier, Will Guilliams, Harry Hay, Mark Horn, Frank Kameny, Michael Kaminer, Jonathon Ned Katz, Robert Kilgore, Paul Kowal, Richard Laermer, Dorr Legg, Steve Levenberg, Phyllis Lyons, Del Martin, Deacon Maccubbin, Ed Mickens, Kendall Morrison, Ann Northrop, Roz Parr, Ron Owen Partners, Clarence Patton, Del Pearce, Victor Ponte, Tom Reilly, Alan Roskoff, Gabriel Rotello, John Sabulis, George Sancoucy, Luc Sante, Henry Scott, Michael Shively, Francis Stevens, Sean Strub, Donald Suggs, Andrew Sullivan, Harry Taylor, Nancy Webster, Urvashi Vaid, Jeff Yarbrough, and numerous people at the International Gay and Lesbian Archives, the Lesbian Herstory Archives, the New York Advertising & Communications Network, Rivendell Marketing, the National Gay Newspaper

Guild, the staff of the 1994 Gay Games, Stonewall Twenty-Five, and the Equality Project.

For their unconditional love and support I'm eternally grateful to: my family, Bill and Lois Wilson and their family, and my father, David Lukenbill—an all-around great guy.

Chapter 1

You Can Bank on It

Marketing has changed. Things are different now, and so are attitudes.

Today, lesbian role models speak for tennis shoe companies, computer manufacturers, and credit card companies. Gay rock stars speak out against unprotected sex. Parents and grandparents are carrying the message of tolerance and acceptance of gay youth to our nation's schools, churches, and synagogues. Even President Clinton spoke at a televised gay and lesbian fund-raising dinner in Washington, hosted by the Human Rights Campaign.

At the New York ceremony of the 1998 Media Awards hosted by GLAAD (Gay and Lesbian Alliance Against Defamation), celebrities such as Sigourney Weaver, k.d. lang, Marlo Thomas, Phil Donahue, and Harvey Weinstein made presentations. They were followed by Tony Bennett, who sang "People" and "Somewhere Over the Rainbow." The star-studded event was also sponsored by big corporate names such as Fannie Mae, AT&T, Sony, IBM, Wells Fargo, and America Online.

Sound acceptable?

Not long ago it sounded silly to many. At least that was the impression among certain Madison Avenue marketing leaders when I suggested in this book's first edition that a "bullish, fast-moving train of economic momentum" was coming thunderously down the track, and that it meant "invigorating market opportunities for businesses and social institutions—both large and small, rural and urban."[1]

That was then. Things are clearer now. "Let Them Wed" demanded an *Economist* cover story complete with two grooms in tuxedos perched on top of a wedding cake.

"Gay Images, Once Kept Out, Are Out Big Time" proclaimed the headline of *The New York Times* Styles section shortly thereafter. And in the past twenty-four months, dozens of industry trade publications including *Advertising Age, Marketing, Business Week, Demographics,* and others have run similar articles confirming that what was once touted merely as trend, has since become commonplace.

Indeed, things are now crystal clear; the gay and lesbian cultural chic of the early 1990s was not a flash in the pan. It was the serious emergence of a new marketplace phenomenon—solid, multifaceted, and growth-oriented.

Today gay and lesbian consumerism has come to be acknowledged—even respected—for its impact on the commercial buying habits of heterosexuals. And though these changes are recent, plenty of gay and lesbian consumers saw the train coming long ago.

Indeed, for them, the signs were everywhere. Perhaps the first real glimpses occurred when heterosexual men's erotic publications began playing up "lesbian sensitivity" in the 1970s. By the late 1980s ACT UP (AIDS Coalition to Unleash Power) not only began getting national exposure, it became a defining catalyst for helping to draw serious, substantive attention to the nation's drug research problems and looming health care crisis.

Those who were skeptical about ACT UP tactics tended to also be those most cynical about the emerging legitimacy of a national gay and lesbian market force. In retrospect, it seems that perhaps more than a few in the American business world were embarrassingly held hostage by Hollywood's original version of who gay people were "supposed to be."

Fortunately, much has changed. What is interesting, though, is that long before debates over same-sex marriage, Boy Scouts, *Ellen, Will & Grace,* or the reemergence of sexual orientation conversion therapy, there was always an economic motivation behind the depiction and positioning of unrealistic homosexual imagery in the commercial marketplace. Basically, it was because there was always a payoff—albeit at the expense of gay and lesbian people (the mass marketing of gay and lesbian stereotypes in television and film all through the twentieth century is well-documented).[2]

For instance, just after the beginning of the twentieth century during the early years of (what is now called) the mental health field, psychiatrists seized upon the opportunity to pontificate about the "sickness" of gay and lesbian people—even legitimizing their stature by making supposedly learned arguments about the dangers of their serving in the military.[3] Of course, that problem is still with us, but the days of finding an automatic payoff at the expense of gays and lesbians have fallen behind us. With the exception of the Conservative Right's disinforming manipulations, the demand for archaic stereotypes of lesbians and gay men as mental misfits, perverts, and moral deviants has evaporated as well. The days of an exclusively heterosexual model of commercial consumption in free enterprise are dead.

Today, a dynamic infusion of opportunity for American marketing continues to invade the entire commercial spectrum—one that is more historic than the appearance of gay male soap opera walk-on characters and more relevant than pictures of nude lesbians in straight male erotica: the power of the domestic gay and lesbian consumer dollar and all that it represents. This power can mean increased revenue for the business you own or work for. It can solidify a shrinking sales database in a company's direct marketing efforts. It can prop up a brand's sagging performance in highly competitive geographic areas. It can even bring credibility to a corporate image in need of one or make a company more attractive for prospective employees, partners and associates, lucrative government contracts—even mergers.

In some industries more than others, a sparkling presence has become all too apparent—one that even some gays and lesbians are completely surprised by. And it has grown right out of their own community: a gay and lesbian cultural and consumer revolution. This revolution is resulting in a seismic shift in popular culture. The effects are already proving to be unavoidable by every large corporation and company with a product to sell or an employee to hire. According to Stephanie Blackwood, a former associate publisher with *The Advocate*, the oldest national gay and lesbian news publication in America, "people [in business] who acknowledge the moral obligation to the gay community are the ones who will ultimately be regarded as the leaders."

What is currently happening is a wholesale change in the spending patterns of millions of American consumers—gay and lesbian as well as heterosexual. And for some companies, their entire way of doing business will alter significantly as a direct result of gay and lesbian buying power and its indirect commercial influence on their existing customer base.

Sound far-fetched? Consider what's been going on recently.

"Big Business Boosts Effort to Win Share of Gay Market" read *The Wall Street Journal* banner headline after a recent Gay and Lesbian Business Expo at the Jacob Javitz Convention Center in New York City "where half of the 225 exhibitors were mainstream companies, up from about one-third of a much smaller group last year said Steven Levenberg, show manager."[4]

At American Airlines, Rick Cirillo, Director of Sales for the Gay and Lesbian Community, says "We [at American Airlines] are happy to be leaders in this area; we allow our gay and lesbian customers to obtain bereavement fares [reduced-fare flights in the event of the death of a domestic partner], and our frequent flyer miles can be used between gay and lesbian domestic partners" (a benefit still only available to married heterosexual couples on other airlines).

Rapid changes regarding gay and lesbian issues in the workplace as well as the marketplace are now apparent in most large telephone companies. According to Bob Baublitz, Market Manager of Ethnic & Premium Marketing & Sales, at Bell Atlantic, "to remain competitive, we have to attract the best and brightest people, we want to be open and acknowledging all our employees. And I think that when you look at gay and lesbian [business issues] from several perspectives, the first being national exposure, the second employee benefits, and the third community sponsorships, we [as a company] are in front."

Indeed, many companies are now out in front, taking the lead, and positioning themselves for the future.

Gay and lesbian buying power is such a commercial and economic force that it is affecting regular decision making at Kodak, IBM, Bristol-Myers Squibb, Hill and Knowlton Public Relations, American Express, Nike, Calvin Klein, Revlon, AT&T, Time Warner, Continental Airlines, Home Box Office, Merrill Lynch, and IKEA. These and other companies are now taking advantage of all the opportunities that exist when corporations pay better attention to sexual diversity in the workplace and in the consumer marketplace. And those companies that get out there first, without hesitation, stand to gain big.

Perhaps that's why more and more marketers from Madison Avenue to Silicon Valley are discussing and negotiating these exciting new realms—from hospital corporations and health clubs in the South to the Biltmore Hotel in Los Angeles and American Marketing Association in New York City. In the recording industry strong niche sales among lesbian consumers can no longer be denied. According to author and New York radio personality Vicki Starr, one of the first out lesbians in American radio, "For years in the country music business there was this belief that women country music artists don't sell. Well, now those people are realizing otherwise."

The word is out with all the television networks, with QVC, Home Shopping Network, Miller Beer, the Republican Party, and the animated halls of Disney; it is impacting media buying for Naya, Evian, and Perrier; it is even stirring within the Catholic Church, affecting politics and rhetoric in the inner sanctums of the Vatican.

Changes in television are apparent in both cable and broadcast realms. "Home Box Office has been top-notch in every way in terms of policies; they are very understanding when it comes to benefits for gay and lesbian employees," says Richard Mayora, account executive for HBO.

And according to Joe Decola, a producer with NBC News, "We are certainly covering more gay and lesbian news now than we were five years ago—in fact, dramatically more. And I would even say somewhat more than just three years ago. In the country overall, there's a cultural change taking place, there are just more people out today—out in media and in the marketplace. That's certainly the case at NBC News—and it all contributes to a growing sense of awareness."

Awareness indeed. Senior-level marketing executives make the same comments at CNN, ABC, and MTV. Savvy business leaders everywhere now agree, gay and lesbian marketing segments are here to stay. And so is the competition for the brand loyalty, the cultural relationships, and of course, the profits.

According to former J. Walter Thompson partner and associate research director, Tony Incalcatera:

Gay and lesbian consumers have come to expect a lot of solicitation from American business. This is now requiring that really smart marketers—meaning cost-efficient and effective marketers—are going to have to start building and helping to transmit specifically focused messages that reach the greatest cross section of consumers as well as other minorities. Not always an easy thing to do. But if advertisers forgo sexual inclusivity, they are going to find themselves in an upstream battle and eventually facing overly diluted brand loyalty.

This book presents the first large-scale accounting of contemporary gay and lesbian consumer culture in America. It provides a fundamental program for understanding gay and lesbian consumers, who they are, and how they differ from the heterosexual mainstream.

It is about how businesses are becoming stronger, more ethical, and more profitable by acknowledging and appealing to an exciting new consumer who is eager to buy but quick to see through smoke and mirrors, hollow rhetoric, and misguided marketing. Untold millions of dollars in industry profits are now at stake for American businesses that position themselves to appeal to these highly specialized consumer market segments. By the turn of the century gross sales in products and services aimed directly at gay and lesbian consumers will be measured in the billions.

According to Steve Bolerjack, co-founder of the gay and lesbian marketing group at Hill and Knowlton Public Relations in New York City, "Businesses today would be wise to begin targeting the gay and lesbian community as a viable market that deserves consideration in the overall mix of business and market planning."

This advice is also echoed by Michael Adams, senior editor for *Successful Meetings,* a trade magazine that follows American business meetings and incentive travel management: "People [in business] are shifting their attitudes. Diversity is now a big issue and the good news is that there are movements going on to include sexual orientation language and consciousness among meetings industry professionals."

Commenting on a recent speaking engagement where he spoke on gay and lesbian issues for the International Association of Exhibit Managers, Adams said, "Giving that [kind of a speech] would have been unheard-of in the 1980s." Yet it was in the early 1980s that gay and lesbian consumers were on the cutting edge of the information superhighway, already communicating over the Internet through soc.motss (Members of the Same Sex), one of the very first on-line bulletin board discussion groups.

Today, things are clearly different. As citizens, gay people know that businesses should be up to speed on sexual orientation issues in the workplace as a matter of moral policy as well as competitive strategy. Only the marketers heeding this call will successfully begin convincing gay and lesbian consumers why they should stay loyal to a company and its brands. The road map for how to do this is in your hands.

RECOGNIZE WHAT IS CHANGING

To begin to understand gay and lesbian consumers is to begin to understand how they have been economically closeted within a marketplace that has been, for the most part, heterosexually oriented for much of this century.

Only in the past twenty years (and especially during the past five) has a truly sophisticated sense of awareness about image and image messaging begun to emerge in marketing with regard to sexual identity. The boundaries continue to change as more companies learn how to push the envelope of commercial aesthetics and social tolerance in pursuit of wider market shares within their respective industries. This dynamic is true across the board: from fashion, advertising, film and television, and the science of direct marketing, to the positioning of beer brands, recorded music, and presidential election campaigns.

America is in a golden era of gay and lesbian visibility. Gay and lesbian Americans are no longer willing to exist within social closets; they are also no longer willing to conform to the confines of yesterday's patriarchal-based marketing paradigms. Erin McHugh, an advertising creative director with Franklin Spier Agency in New York City, agrees, stating: "I think it's fair to say that the history of advertising and marketing in general has been largely centered around heterosexual archetypes."

That is what is changing. Today gay and lesbian people are out—not only as individuals—but as families, people of faith, teachers, celebrity entertainers, and youth activists. They are also becoming much more informed as consumers, as well as employees and investors. And they are learning to expect companies to communicate a sense of awareness and comprehensive understanding of who they are and who they are not.

These important developments require contemporary-minded marketing professionals—and corporate leaders in general—to begin to nurture the amplification of sexual identity within the landscape of commercial imagery. In other words, to allow a wider, more realistic range of America's spiritual and emotional character to be explored in relationship to sexual orientation, personal identity, and how they relate to product marketing.

Ultimately, this requires business to adopt an understanding and ability to reengineer company management policies on gay and lesbian workplace policy as well as marketplace policy and changing consumer ethics. It also requires that advertising leaders revisit their notions of what constitutes real niche market research and "appropriate" visual and stylistic mirroring in the creative development of visual arts. It requires that new things be tried, that boundaries be pushed and that new messages be communicated to express inclusiveness, understanding, and validation of America's emerging pansexual culture—which brings us to the subject of "code."

COMING OUT WITH THE CODE

All around us in popular culture is code—social code, sexual code, image code. Code is about creating "doublespeak." Some of it is obvious; some of it is crafty. Advertising in particular is all about code and the sending of pluralistic messages. So is political posturing, which makes use of code with the so-called "sound bite." In the response to our sound-bitten information age, the news media attempts to break down the code, but all too often ends up creating more code because news itself is a product, requiring its own standard of coding.

Gay and lesbian code in the 1980s and early 1990s was about manipulating perception and playing to gay (mostly male) sensibility in visual imagery and planting mixed message ideas in printed consumer language. It was about the shrewd and persistent use of sexually ambiguous advertising in a heterosexually focused mass culture. It happened in politics as well.

Watered-down, disingenuous phrases such as alternative lifestyles, longtime companions, lifelong partners, personal confidante, personal lifestyle choice, and so on began to be used as a way of suggesting that single folks might also be nonheterosexual folks.

Fashion ads showed handsome, romantic-looking guys close together with playful facial expressions that could be read by consumers as homosexually suggestive or merely indicating "a close friendship."

Early on, when this kind of code was used constructively to reach gay and lesbian consumers—meaning metaphorically, and in the proper cultural context—it was the gay-oriented advertiser's single most important tool. It was a formula to lock in brand identity and communicate a broad sense of individual inclusion across gay and lesbian consumer groups, as well as heterosexual ones. Unfortunately, the vast use of gay code came to be just as exploitive and disruptive as a lot of other advertising.

What we have today is a virtual soup of sexual exploitation covering everything from diet to underwear. For instance, when code is used by the food and beverage industry, we see it as the aggressive marketing of fat-free products with subtext suggestions of the desirability that comes from being overly thin. It whispers, "Don't be like those people who have a weight problem." Modern food and beverage advertising is loaded with sexual suggestion and the promise of physical satisfaction, all in an effort to push processed, mass-produced foodstuff. It is particularly apparent in the presentation of desserts and fat-free products, but is even used in the presentation of "premium" cat foods. In the 1990s, the way many edible products are currently being photographed oozing, dripping, and steaming across consumers' lips, tongues, and fingers would have resulted in disgust and outrage just a few years ago. Today hunger is coded as an overly primal desire and presented in nearly lewd contexts designed to create a delusional promise of hypersatiation. It is all coding, though, designed to play on a number of insecurities based upon need, desire, and an oversexualized sense of fulfillment and personal satisfaction about life.

With the coding has come an increase in portion sizes of packaged foods and beverages. In the 1960s the average soft drink was six ounces. Today it is sixteen ounces in cans and bottles and thirty-two ounces in convenience store "to go" cups marketed under such names as "Big Gulp" and "Extra Grande."

Indeed, today, the synthetic fat with the brand name Olean passes marketing (and, questionably, the FDA) muster with consumers who are willing to buy a product with a warning label about potential *abdominal cramps, loose stools, and disrupted vitamin absorption.* We have come to accept this as easily as we have health warnings on cigarette labels, artificial sweeteners, microwaves, and gasoline pumps.

But what has really resulted? A nation more obese.

The irresponsible use of coded messaging by corporate (and political) market forces runs through the entire twentieth century and is now more pervasive at every level of society than ever before in the history of capitalism. It is widely responsible for the amplification of minority stereotyping among less educated people—particularly with regard to gay and lesbian Americans, their alleged wealth, and their often-perceived status as people "wanting special rights."

Radio talk show hosts, alone, have increased their own marketability by spreading and focusing on erroneous, unsubstantiated characterizations of gay people. They are held responsible for everything from the breakdown of family structures and the decline of morality, to being part of a radical left-wing "agenda" that seeks to destroy America's "traditional" heritage.

In *Race Matters,* Cornel West wrote about the challenges specifically facing black cultural institutions in America:

> Corporate market institutions have contributed greatly to their collapse . . . that complex set of interlocking enterprises that have a disproportionate amount of capital [and] power, and exercise a disproportionate influence on how our society is run and how our culture is shaped. Needless to say, the primary motivation of these institutions is to make profits, and their basic strategy is to convince the public to consume. These institutions have helped create a seductive way of life, a culture of consumption that capitalizes on every opportunity to

make money. Market calculations and cost-benefit analyses hold sway in almost every sphere of U.S. society. The common denominator of these calculations and analyses is usually the provision, expansion, and intensification of *pleasure.* . . . The reduction of individuals to objects and pleasure is especially evident in the culture industries—television, radio, video, music—in which gesture of sexual foreplay and orgiastic pleasure flood the marketplace.[5]

Ironically, gay and lesbian consumers are especially aware of these forces because they still don't see genuine gay-identified "orgiastic pleasure" flooding the marketplaces where they shop. But they have seen plenty of coded messages. And there is an increasing indication that they are tired of them.

The Agenda of Code

When gay or lesbian advertising code is reduced to its skeletal structure, it is always about selling ideas and communicating positions. It has traditionally been mixed, subliminal, at times disingenuous, and at times validating—but rarely completely trustworthy. A few years ago it was used by Burroughs Wellcome in their $25 million advertising campaign designed to get people (particularly gay men) to start taking the drug AZT. The campaign—which ran widely in gay publications and in outdoor advertising placed in gay neighborhoods—focused on health and the importance of getting tested for HIV, which is a responsible message. But the coded subtext was about getting people to take the drug AZT should they test positive for the HIV virus.[6] This was done before the efficacy of the drug's ability to prolong life was even remotely accepted as legitimate among most gay men. Its worth is still contested by some today.

Call gay advertising (or any other advertising) code what you like—sinister doublespeak, corporate public relations, brand loyalty development, or simple relationship marketing—it is all profit-based, marketplace messaging. And it is all used to get you to change your mind about something relating to your purchasing behavior regardless of reality, and often in denial of solid facts, personal intuition, and overall human nature.

Confront any management executive or brand manager of nearly any popular product in America about its coded advertising motivations and psychology and you will get even more code. Spin. Public relations. The prepackaged package. Politicians do it. Lawyers do it. People in job interviews do it.

Yet few mainstream companies or advertising agencies successful at attracting and keeping gay and lesbian consumers for their clients will admit that any kind of code has been their mainstay. Of those that will, even fewer will elaborate on the details. But being able to use code (specifically in the pursuit of gay and lesbian consumers) has been one of the most important tools that have worked up until now. Some of the better copywriters, artists, and photographers have known all along just exactly how to go about using code.

In fact, many advertising executives, and certainly most consumers, would be hard pressed to identify or crack the code whenever it shows up in marketing imagery. But gay consumers know it when they see it and they call it "gaydar"—a kind of sixth sense, an intuition about gender-specific sensuality, artistic sensibility, and cultural archetypes.

At times, heterosexual consumers notice it as the "androgynous look"—however, many gay and lesbian consumers are insulted by its use if it is sprinkled around too carelessly by companies that have traditionally been less than supportive of gay rights. But the androgynous look is only a small part of the kind of coding that is necessary to appeal to gay consumers today.

The Politics of Code

Two important facts surround the use of code in our evolving marketplace. The first is that same-sex advertising code (imagery that can potentially be perceived by a consumer as gay/lesbian or straight) simply makes it into broad cross sections of American advertising whether it is done on purpose or not. The second is that same-sex imagery is now beginning to be used to sell products precisely because it can be taken so many ways without being seen as necessarily single or married, exclusively straight or exclusively gay or lesbian.

Communicating an unspoken assumption about one's sexual orientation in advertising imagery is critical in not alienating gay consumers. This fact is something Madison Avenue folks don't like to talk about—usually for one or two simple reasons: the appointed individuals speaking on behalf of the company (gay or straight) might not be courageous enough to candidly discuss actual gay and lesbian market issues with authority; or they want to protect their prized secrets on how they came to attract and keep their gay and lesbian consumer following.

Patrick Lehman, a New York-based visuals and image design consultant who has advised everyone in the advertising and fashion world from Calvin Klein to Kmart, has very strong ideas about what informs and makes the use of code effective when targeting gays and lesbians—particularly as consumers of clothing and fashion:

> Twenty-five years ago, you had five magazines in America. We sold ourselves on a single culture. Today our culture is broader, longer, and more diverse. People who read *Vibe, Esquire,* or *The Advocate* may still read a fitness magazine, an industry trade publication and the local newspaper because you can't get everything in one place any more. So as a designer I have to do something to cut through the noise. And when it comes to gay and lesbian people, I find that they'll always buy "clever" even though it may not be exclusively aimed at them. Generally, I think that any kind of advertising in any industry that is hip, ironic, or contains a little attitude, sarcasm, or bitchiness is what gay people will click onto. Often gay and lesbian people have a certain bitterness from being oppressed by mainstream society. So by being on the outside looking in, for so long, many of them actually revel a little in things that are really "arch" or a little on the sneering side. But that's only part of the picture. Good compelling imagery also has to be exciting, electric, and stimulating to different people for different reasons, but it all has to happen at once—as an ensemble of feeling. It's hard to always boil it down to a specific formula. And it doesn't always have to be sexually suggestive. But turning up the heat and widening the panorama of sexual tension is definitely something everybody tries to do and the unfolding of more gay and lesbian con-

sciousness is simply part of that evolution in marketing. Not everyone wants to admit it, but that's exactly what's going on.

Advertising professionals on the account side of the business are especially nervous about admitting that they are marketing homo-erotic sexual tension—particularly in relation to their tactical strategy and positioning of a product against an aggressive competitor. This is because gay and lesbian publishers and advertising directors (especially employees at large advertising agencies) have known that up until recently there has been no industrial or commercial playing field littered with more social taboos, corporate minefields, and political booby traps than the gay and lesbian marketplace. In addition, getting a senior-level manager at a large company or advertising agency to sign paperwork for actual advertising buys in gay and lesbian media has never been an easy task either. But, almost as if to overcompensate, their creative departments routinely produce some of the most homoerotic imagery imaginable. In fact, more of it was seen throughout the 1980s than in the rest of the decades of this century combined. But until recently, as Lehman acknowledges, nearly everyone was afraid to talk about it.

A MELTING POT OF CODED MESSAGING

For years fashion advertising never appeared in gay and lesbian magazines, but the marketing firms and advertising agencies contracted to produce and place commercial imagery for the fashion industry did everything but acknowledge that gay people were part of the overall mix of people being targeted through the mainstream. And a cursory glance through any *GQ* or *Cosmopolitan* magazine during the last quarter of this century bears testament to the fashion and advertising industry's ongoing fetishistic affair with same-sex imagery.

This trend toward sexual inclusiveness continues and is now apparent in nearly all industries that make use of mainstream advertising—and, finally, more and more media buys are beginning to be made in gay and lesbian publications. Today, American advertising (and media imagery in general) abounds with more mixed signals and subtly woven homoerotic imagery—for both men and women—than ever before.

This imagery does not exist as a conspiratorial agreement between model, photographer, stylist, and media buyer. It is simply now part of an overall understanding and acceptance of a changing consumer marketplace by perceptive, leading-edge companies that recognize that lesbians and gay men are part of their sales base and, in fact, can be reached through the mainstream if approached with the right messaging and an appropriate level of sensitivity that does not distract or dilute heterosexual interest. This is especially noticeable in the increased and highly sophisticated depiction of a more generalized sensuality which is often being blended with a looser attitude about human nudity.

According to Vincent Boucher, a New York creative director and fashion stylist with ten plus years experience in the development of some of America's most important visual imagery,

> . . . advertising is sexier than it was twenty years ago—today it can cut both ways, playing to straight audiences and gay audiences at the same time. Today there's a broadening of scope about who's going to be "brought in" by advertising. It's really an evolution that started in the 1980s with photographers, and now the body itself has become such a totem. Although nudity by itself does not have a gay connotation in our society, it can still be used to pull in a gay audience—as can an ironic stance, for instance, or a kind of humor that is wry and urban. When designers get together to do a shoot we don't sit down and say, "OK, is this going to appeal to a gay audience?" It may get commented on from time to time but it's really now just part of the package. I don't think "gay" has to be discussed, but I do think people are thinking about it now. It's an accepted part of the job that you have to appeal to all audiences.

Indeed, all it takes to see what Boucher is talking about is a simple look around the country at the way we have come to accept more and more sexualized imagery in advertising over the past decade. It is widely apparent in dozens of consumer industries—particularly in the marketing of fashion, men's underwear, alcohol, blue jeans, cigarettes, automobiles, bath soap, and fabric softener.

The liquor industry has become particularly adept at signaling its desire to communicate to all consumers—straight, as well as gay and lesbian. Consider a recent Dewar's Scotch advertisement that plays on a number of suggestions about sex and the taboo of discussing male anatomy. The advertisement was particularly unbelievable— even to gay men (see photo insert section). Interestingly, it plays to all audiences. It also toys with the brazen without being too suggestive of behavior or sexual fantasy.

Underwear continues to get a lot of play in American media lately—both men's and women's. But for the longest time there was only a focus on women's underwear—or better yet, women's underwear-buying habits, since they also influenced men's underwear decisions. But what other consumer group was Calvin Klein playing to when he blazoned the near-nude body of the handsome and muscular young Marky Mark across the sides of buses and billboards all over America just a few short seasons ago?

It is highly unlikely that many heterosexual men were sexually turned on by a young white male with perfect washboard abdominal muscles wearing double-digit-priced Calvin Klein underwear. They might, on some level, have fantasized about themselves being as young, physically fit, and attractive as Marky Mark and therefore more attractive to women. But there were no women in many of the shots with him. So was the heterosexual male supposed to take a leap of faith in the fantasy? This kind of aggressiveness in selling male clothing was certainly never a trend in selling beer, sports cars, or certain colognes to men. Nor has it ever been the approach used to sell products in much of the advertising seen in *Sports Illustrated*—a decidedly male-focused publication.

So who else was buying the underwear besides all those heterosexual men who aren't married or in an intimate enough relationship to receive the gift of underwear from a woman? And what was the symbolism behind Marky Mark's bashful smile and his hand placed between his legs?

Translation: Yes, I'm attractive to many American women. And, yes, I know you (gay) men find me attractive, but I'm straight and you can't have what I have. So I'll literally create a boundary here between you and me and my sense of maleness by covering myself with my hand. Oh, you can continue to look, because I'm paid to let you. But looking is all that's allowed. Just be sure to pick up a package the next time you're in the store and think of me.

According to Lehman, who was working for Calvin Klein at the time, Marky Mark "was a perfect universal object of desire. He was a fantasy for many gay men because he represented the unattainable man (being straight), yet for women he was young and cuddly; the adorable boylike man you want to hug."

Brilliant advertising? Yes. And brilliant use of multilevel coding as well.

Calvin Klein underwear is still popular among many gay men across the country—most of whom, it is safe to say, do not have many women buying their undergarments for them. Interestingly enough, the Calvin Klein underwear campaign that followed the Marky Mark campaign did, in fact, incorporate a female model undressing a male model—but only after it was ascertained that a trend could be set by appealing to a certain market segment of male youth through mixed messaging.

Since that time, Donna Karan has gotten into the underwear act, as well. But she has actually gone a step further than Calvin Klein: she installed domestic partner benefits for her gay and lesbian employees—something that is not only good business practice, but sends a certain message as well.

How about a recent advertising campaign for Virginia Slims cigarettes? Remember the one that showed the two young female subjects staring into each other's eyes while sitting very close together at a sidewalk cafe? They both had glorious smiles on their faces—as though they really enjoyed each other's company or perhaps had just shared an intimate secret. The headline read, "The most important thing about a break is who you take it with."

READING THE FUTURE BETWEEN THE LINES

In downtown New York City, a Guess? billboard advertisement shows three GQ-looking white men sitting in the front seat of a convertible looking over their shoulders toward the camera's view, which is behind the car. There are no women in the shot and no one is in the back seat.

Does Guess? think that heterosexual men are attracted to three young men who ride together in the front seat of an automobile? How many straight men in America—especially that young—would feel comfortable riding in the front seat of any car with two other guys, when there is plenty of room in the back—especially if they are single and in a convertible?

This ad was very revealing: it put a certain kind of man and his friends in the front seat looking back at everyone else who was left behind. But who was it really putting in the driver's seat? And who was it telling that it's okay to cruise together, out in the open, ahead of everyone else?

Madonna was one of the first major performers to blanket America with sexual code—code used specifically to appeal to the entire panorama of sexual expression. This was especially obvious to gay and lesbian consumers. Many of the artists and industry professionals Madonna works with are gay or lesbian, and a healthy portion of her talent developed and became popular as it emerged from the downtown New York club scene—which is very gay.

Madonna learned about and utilized a real part of her experience with gay and lesbian culture as one of the ways to propel many of her more popular artistic ideas. It is no wonder that she is widely adored by gay men and particularly respected by many American lesbians for her independence, courage, and self-actualization as a woman.

She also gave many talk show hosts the encouragement they needed to delve into everything from lesbian love confessions to "hunk-o-rama fashion updates" complete with near-nude fashion shows of muscle-studded young men with bulging crotches and pearly white smiles parading in front of camera to the sounds of downtown New York City mixed house music.

Then came the (already nostalgic) *Roseanne* comedy skits—particularly the corner-turning "lesbian kiss" episode with Ms. Hemingway. It was one of the most-watched shows of the television season and a near-perfect and direct use of marketing code that resulted in increased audience share and a continued loyalty to Roseanne and her character among a broad cross section of television viewers. Including such scripting ensured gay and lesbian viewership, and it communicated a sense of social brazenness during prime time when the most profit could be realized. But it was really just the tip of the iceberg when it came to gay and lesbian imagery. In retrospect, it was a taste of the television content that was around the corner for American audiences. Since that time some thirty regular or semiregular lesbian or gay television characters have become commonplace in both daytime and prime time television viewing slots.

Today we have an ongoing cross-dressing fad in marketing that was first tried out in teenage-oriented commercials on Saturday mornings for everything from bubble gum and soda pop to basketball shoes and breakfast cereal, but it all had a few cultural roots in gay male theater. And interestingly, it all developed—almost simultaneously—alongside the VH-1 Music Television sensation, RuPaul.

Then Ellen came out. The code was broken. There was significant controversy. And even though her show was eventually canceled, she left behind over two dozen recurring lesbian and gay television characters. No more controversy—there had been a sea change.

Today, the mayor of New York City has buttressed his popular appeal and perhaps even his long-term political capital by appearing in drag in public and on a recent *Saturday Night Live* skit in which he was the host.

His appearance was not so much sexual coding as it was cultural coding—a mere nod acknowledging his understanding of "camp sensitivity" and a show of willingness to be one of the guys as well as one of the funky crowd that understands nuance and diversity messaging.

But marketing analysts and political strategists saw it for what it was: a grand plan to develop and widen Giuliani brand identity and voter loyalty in the minds of young television viewers and future national election voters. It's the same thing Bill Clinton did with a saxophone.

If you are now saying to yourself, "Oh, puh-leeaze," you might want to consider that the expression itself has long been a stereotypical lament among older gay men and actually became infused into popular culture by gay situation comedy writers in New York and Los Angeles in the 1970s. It's now a routine expression used by everyone from Joan Rivers and David Letterman to schoolteachers and politicians.

SEEING IS BELIEVING

The long and short of all of this, of course, is change, with gay- and lesbian-oriented imagery becoming more a regular part of the mainstream—in commercial media as well as national politics. In addition, less of it is purposefully coded, more of it is now appropriately inclusive or directly communicated without reservation.

Some of the first nationwide indications of this phenomenon began in the early 1980s with the development of gay and lesbian sections in large city bookstores. Today nearly every major bookstore chain outlet across the United States has a section specifically allocated to gay- and lesbian-oriented books. Bookstore managers have simply learned that gay and lesbian consumers are a critical segment of their overall customer base.

There are now just as many advertiser-supported gay and lesbian magazines on America's newsstands as there are fashion magazines. And both gay and non-gay market sectors are now playing to each other in an attempt to cover as much competitive editorial ground as possible.

National lesbian and gay magazines such as *OUT, Genre, Curve, Girl Friends, Frontiers, The Advocate, Icon,* and others have all made a regular habit of putting popular heterosexual celebrities on their covers, while *Details, Esquire, GQ, POZ,* and even *Playboy* have begun incorporating gay-themed stories or angles in an attempt to compete for the demanding, more evolved reader.

Despite *Ellen*'s cancellation, groundbreaking television presentations in America including *Will & Grace, South Park, The Simpsons, Roseanne, Frazier, Friends, Mad About You,* and the PBS airing of *In the Life* and *Tales of the City,* all benefited enormously from their decision to incorporate a clear level of visibility for gay or lesbian characters and subjects within their plot lines.

MTV now transmits the words, images, metaphors, and symbols of a gay- and lesbian-infused culture on the hour every hour into 80 percent of American households—every single day. The music video sensations of megastars such as the Indigo Girls, Madonna, Prince, Janet Jackson, Sting, and others all garner strong gay and lesbian followings based on their socially conscious lyrics and sensitivity to a cultural diversity that embraces all groups.

Numerous celebrities including Martina Navratilova, Elton John, k.d. lang, Melissa Etheridge, even prime-time Fox Television's *Married with Children* star Amanda Bearse have all come out as gay public figures with great fanfare. And each realized an almost immediate increase in ratings, popularity, record sales, and ability to communicate a moral sense of political and social responsibility to their fans by virtue of being more open about who they are and what their work can be about.

Of course, entertainment industry producers are all thrilled as well. They know something dramatic is happening—something they can all take to the bank.

REAL PEOPLE AND THE REAL WORLD

Years have now passed since the death of MTV's *The Real World* star Pedro Zamora, who was out, gay, HIV positive, and in a relationship with another man. Before he died, he was featured on the cover of *POZ*, a competently edited national magazine aimed at everyone concerned or affected by HIV and AIDS.

Pedro was the first contemporary gay public figure to be eulogized by a sitting president. And nearly every television story that covered Pedro's life was presented sensitively, frankly, and unsensationally. Quite a change since the days of Rock Hudson.

Of course, reruns of *The Real World* continue to air. And so do the reminders that the interior furnishings for the show were provided by IKEA in exchange for promotional announcements. IKEA was the first home furnishings company to run an advertisement on television purposely showing two clearly out, gay men buying a coffee table together. And savvy gay male teenagers are quite aware of the MTV *Real World*/IKEA connection.

The IKEA commercial and the death of Pedro Zamora was perhaps the first time the American television-viewing public was confronted with the lives of today's gay and lesbian generation: literally real people such as Pedro, and real people such as the gentlemen in the IKEA advertisement were presented matter-of-factly—without sensation, and in retrospect without any real controversy.

Being gay was no longer limited to America being bludgeoned with HIV-infected Rock Hudson pictures on the cover of the *National Enquirer*. It was now about acceptance. Being real. Seeing real people living real lives in the real world.

The corner definitely had been turned by the time *The New Yorker* magazine ran a gay marriage cover—something its then-editor, Tina Brown, rightly sensed to be a sign of the times.

Since that time Martina Navratilova has been a celebrity model for Apple Computer. An Apple Computer advertisement showing Martina holding her PowerBook while standing next to wide receiver Art Monk has appeared on the inside front cover of numerous magazines including *OUT.*

Today direct marketing aimed at gay and lesbian consumers has become common because it offers many companies a way of testing the waters before going into high-profile advertising campaigns through print media. Even gay and lesbian consumers are not always aware that many of the catalogues they receive in the mail were sent to them specifically because they are believed to be gay or lesbian by companies doing the direct marketing.

MOVING AHEAD

Right now, companies that want to obtain, keep, and develop better, more profitable consumer relationships with heterosexual and gay and lesbian Americans need to start learning, investigating, planning, and speaking to gay and lesbian consumers in a more contemporary way: in their language, on their turf, and without corporate self-consciousness and, most important, without the closeted economic straitjackets of the past. Communicating a company's awareness of gay and lesbian diversity actually positions it as socially conscious, thereby increasing its brand loyalty among heterosexual consumers as well.

The time for heavily coded gay and lesbian imagery is nearing its end. Directly communicating in the mainstream marketplace to gay and lesbian consumers is where the market trend is now. And companies that are willing to update their nondiscrimination policy statements, implement full domestic partnership benefits for their gay and lesbian employees, and then proceed to be more direct about who it is that they are targeting in the marketplace will be the ones to benefit not only first, but in the long haul.

One of the most beautifully produced advertisements aimed at lesbians exclusively comes from Olivia Cruises—a travel and vacation destination service for gay women. It unabashedly shows two women embracing on the beach in much the way Madison Avenue has stylistically portrayed heterosexual intimacy since the 1950s. This ad is a spectacular example of gay (more specifically, lesbian) advertising at its best—devoid of ambiguity and aggressive exploitation.

Of course, not all advertising is required to be completely gay or completely heterosexual to be effective. But, increasingly, neither can companies afford to continue to act as if the world is completely heterosexual—or even asexual.

More of corporate America, its human resource managers, and its marketing representatives must learn to speak directly to lesbians and gay men. Those in business who refuse to do this, who refuse to treat gays and lesbians in the workplace as equals, or who put up barriers against them in the marketplace, only risk diluted brand loyalty and possible harassment lawsuits against them.

However, for corporate leaders that pay attention, there is a big payoff for conducting business with this genuinely new and exciting consumer marketplace.

But being a leader means more than just being willing to target a new market niche. Real corporate leaders accept that sexual diversity matters—both in the marketplace and the workplace. Going for profits from gay or lesbian consumers without delivering equally in the workplace is not advised.

The future is about moving toward more openness: in markets, in planning, and in treatment of gays and lesbians. The future is about accepting that gay and lesbian consumers and workers are good for business—the kind of business you can take to the bank.

Chapter 2

Visibility:
The New Politics of Profit

The lifeblood of free enterprise comprises many things: capital, liberty, equal opportunity, organizational independence—but perhaps, most important, visibility.

Capitalism thrives on the shrewd manipulation of compelling imagery. So does the equal rights movement for gay and lesbian citizens. Gay and lesbian freedom marches and pride celebrations are all about the same issues: liberty, equal opportunity, independence, organization, and visibility.

In the early 1990s, commercial imagery in America began fundamentally changing across our entire media-drenched landscape. For over 200 years, the mere acknowledgement of gay and lesbian people in American society was virtually nonexistent. This "nonexistence" was amplified in mainstream advertising and television media throughout the last hundred years. In many areas of the country, any allusions to same-sex affection were considered forbidden, immoral, or outright illegal.

Of those references to same-sex affection that did occasionally occur in television and film, most were of a highly stereotypical nature or were presented in less-than-accurate contexts—usually for the gratuitous consumption of what were assumed to be heterosexual audiences. Outside of the print advertisements seen in the gay and lesbian press or occasional tokenism in television dramas about "being different" or living with AIDS, accurate gay and lesbian imagery was rarely projected through mass media with any degree of consistency until the late 1980s.

Today, things are changing. Even though the history of the gay and lesbian emancipation movement has been a fight for equal protection, the fair application of laws, public visibility, and the general public's acceptance of their moral legitimacy, as a group gay people are developing more than a political identity. They are in fact developing an economic and commercial identity as well as a cultural, philanthropic, and spiritual one.

Gay and lesbian consciousness is growing—rapidly. Today, gay and lesbian consumers are ubiquitously aware of the sexual and affectional inaccuracies that persist in the mainstream's portrayal of their culture. They are aware of which religious figures embrace and support their causes and which ones do not. They are learning which business corporations are on their side and which ones are not. And perhaps, most keenly, they have finely tuned levels of emotional radar when it comes to the proliferation of unbalanced or inaccurate images of their contemporaries in commercial imagery. They see through the doublespeak of politicians and gratuitous pandering of corporations.

One thing is certain—gay and lesbian consumers see how visual imbalances and misrepresentations of gay people in society are largely responsible for the antigay violence in the neighborhoods where they live. They see how routine censorship of real issues and values ultimately breeds contempt and ignorance in the populace—further preventing the passage of equal rights legislation and the establishment of antidiscrimination codes at the municipal level.

According to writer and veteran lesbian activist Ann Northrop:

> There is a real misunderstanding of who we are. And then there's an assumption that we have made a choice—a sinful, disgusting, perverted choice that is about lifestyle. There's a lack of understanding that we [gay and lesbian people] have an essential nature, and that the world is a diverse place sexually and that we have been discriminated against through misunderstanding and lack of education [of the public at large].

Ever conscious of these imbalances, gay and lesbian consumers pay closer-than-average attention to nearly every public policy issue that comes up for review. They are also more likely to have a heightened awareness and interest in corporate equal employment opportunity issues, and are usually more aware than their colleagues of antidiscrimination policies affecting their positions in the workplace. There is also increasing evidence that younger gays and lesbians vote more regularly and pay more attention to election-year political rhetoric.

Some of the most compelling evidence of this notion is chronicled in an important paper authored by Murray Edelman, PhD, editorial director of the Voter News Service, a national consortium of the major television networks and the Associated Press.[1] In his paper, Edelman cites exit poll research conducted during the 1992 presidential election by Voter Research and Surveys (VRS). The survey found that 71 percent of gay men and 69 percent of lesbians were under the age of 45 compared to 56 percent of straight men and 58 percent of straight women. What was striking was that most of the difference was found in the eighteen to twenty-nine age group.

Overall, the research data estimated the size of the national gay and lesbian vote to be about 3.2 percent of the population. A *Los Angeles Times* poll conducted during the same time period was 3 percent—"an usually close agreement for two totally independent surveys," states Edelman.

These findings shed interesting light on just how engaged America's younger gay and lesbian generation really is and how willing they are to self-identify in comparison to their more senior peers. It also helps explain why they are more sensitive to the integrity of news broadcasts during the annual gay and lesbian marches for equal rights (held each June in commemoration of New York City's Stonewall Riots of 1969).

The currently maturing generation of gay and lesbian Americans is simply more visible and paying more attention to the business of conducting business and how it relates to their lives. And therein lies the opportunity for profit for companies that plan accordingly and with responsibility.

STRONG MEDICINE FOR CORPORATE AMERICA

For America's companies to conduct business with gay and lesbian consumers today is to confront the politics, challenges, and issues they face as citizens. Consumer goods manufacturers, corporate leaders, and advertising executives not willing to accept this reality would be better off closing this book, investing their marketing dollars in other

niche segments or corporate mutual funds, while hoping against hope
that their clients and competitors don't continue reading.

In the evolving, increasingly politicized global consumer marketplace, gay and lesbian customers continue to signal as a group that
they are more aware, more in-tune, and more willing to combine
their politics with their discretionary spending for goods and services than ever before. This increased strength and heightened visibility draws even more attention to their worldwide importance as
consumers in a changing marketplace. This visibility has captured
the attention of airlines and credit cards as well as foreign car
manufacturers.

In the past eighteen months American gay and lesbian publications have begun focusing more closely on gay and lesbian marketing, economic, and consumer issues. And more gay and lesbian
nonprofit groups, political action committees, and activist groups
have begun building coalitions around marketplace issues. Through
gay and lesbian newspapers and magazines, on-line computer networks, and corporate affinity relationships, gay and lesbian consumers are now tracking corporate America's relationship to them
on a level unprecedented in the country's history.

This heightened interest in the policies of America's companies
both large and small is exceptionally serious among gay and lesbian
consumers. And the reality is that these facts can be used to a
company's advantage (provided their own house is order) or they
can result in a public relations nightmare that can take years to
mend with gay and lesbian consumers if not taken seriously when
the opportunity presents itself.

That opportunity is now, particularly in light of the fact that
acceptance of sexual diversity in American society is significantly
more widespread than ever before. Figure 2.1 confirms the steady,
systematic decline in prejudicial attitudes toward gay and lesbian
people across the United States over the past fifteen years.[2]

At the current rate of change as indicated above, the majority of
Americans across the country will be overwhelmingly in support of
some kind of same-sex marriage legislation in the very near future.
Sooner or later there will be a federal statute on equality issues
pertaining to gay and lesbian Americans in housing, employment,
and access to spousal benefits. Any American corporation that does

FIGURE 2.1. Percentage of Population Who Would Prefer Not to Be Around Gay People

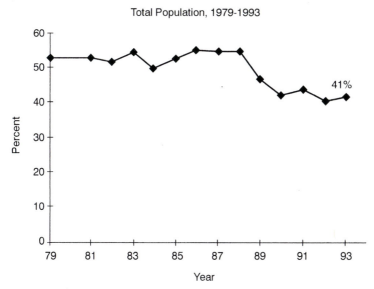

Total Population, 1979-1993

Source: Yankelovich MONITOR 1994.

not at least have a policy banning discrimination based on sexual orientation will soon find itself among increasingly extremist company in the eyes of gay and lesbian consumers—and soon heterosexual consumers as well.

Thousands of American companies are already (often at the advice of their legal counsel) finding themselves backpedaling on their outdated employee hiring policies and scrambling to put out routine public relations fires, all in the name of poor planning or pending lawsuits.

Regarding this specific issue, many companies are already realizing that this absolutely painless step (often a mere rewording of their employee manuals) actually translates to a wise, long-term investment eventually affecting their ability to attract loyal employees and sell stock and products. Senior-level executives who stand in the way of these changes in America's workplace ethics do so at their company's competitive peril.

REFOCUSING THE IMAGES

Whenever an attractive or newly supportive portrayal of gay men or lesbians occurs in a magazine ad, a newspaper article, a television situation comedy plot, or direct-mail advertising campaign, rest assured, gay and lesbian consumers take notes, talk, and keep mental diaries. They gravitate more readily toward any positive accentuation of sexual orientation in media and commercial enterprise—because until recently, they rarely saw themselves accurately portrayed.

Until recently, wherever gay and lesbian Americans looked (at least outside predominantly gay neighborhoods) all they saw was imagery that could always be argued as nothing more than heterosexually intended imagery. Even most fashion advertising aimed exclusively at men made use of the obligatory woman in the photograph's construction—much the way advertising made use of the token racial minority in the advertising of the 1960s.

Discerning which companies and advertising agencies were making use of any degree of code to quietly reach gay and lesbian consumers was difficult in the past because the use of code always had to be, on some level, deniable. It wasn't until recently that public relations departments began spinning their advertising campaign visuals as being aimed at all consumers of all walks of life.

Still, there were a number of critical incidents throughout the past ten years that helped to rally gay and lesbian consumers toward a more focused analysis of products and services, marketing tactics, and the use of commercial imagery in general.

One of the more recent and most infamous examples, the early Nut 'n' Honey cereal commercials, actually typified the advertising industry's history of ignorance and insensitivity to gay and lesbian Americans. The commercial showed two cowboys placing guns next to the head of another who said the name of the cereal but was heard to say the double entendre, "nothing, honey." This suggested that he was not only gay, but stereotypically prissy, effeminate, and therefore of a perverted enough character that they should protect themselves from his alleged degeneracy by threatening him with murder by simultaneous gunshot wounds to both sides of his head.

Suggesting that gay and lesbian Americans are sick people, monsters who use prissy language that will contaminate the morals of the masses and are therefore worthy of death is a classic strategy used by religious radicals and political extremists to this day. Still, it is almost unbelievable that such advertising actually made it onto national television within the past few years.

This may be a small example, but we must remember that modern communication culture is cabled, radio talk-showed, and Nightlined into a *Larry King Live,* Howard Sterned mass of lukewarm cynicism. Heterosexuality is still the norm in media, and a commercial such as that for Nut 'n' Honey may seem mildly humorous to the uninformed—merely reminiscent of old western skepticism—but it is seen by gay consumers as a frightening reminder of society's history of intolerance for the humanity of the homosexual public.

The frequent distortion or outright censoring of the existence of gay and lesbian culture in modern life, in advertising imagery, books, and general media, combined with the occasional cultural bashing of gay and lesbian people through commercials such as Nut 'n' Honey, simply forced gay and lesbian consumers to constantly make allowances and readjustments in their minds for heterosexual society's image-producing inaccuracies.

Even though times are changing and television producers and movie directors are beginning to be more inclusive of gay and lesbian culture, another reality remains as well. In many areas of the United States, gay and lesbian consumers are not at all represented in mainstream advertising imagery. Subconsciously, they have to imagine themselves recreated in too many American marketing campaigns, transposing their very wants, desires, values, sense of humor, and basic human feelings into the heterosexually intended imagery.

In other words, they have to, on some level, recreate the pictures to suit their own sense of perspective on the world. And of course, one's sexual orientation greatly affects one's perspective. It's asking the consumer to do a lot of work.

Certainly, different consumers experience varying degrees of fantasy and context recreation when exposed to different kinds of advertising. But with the exception of the ambiguous, ever-changing world of fashion advertising, gay and lesbian consumers have to take most advertising in America a few steps further for it to have any relevance to their lives. A gay or lesbian consumer admiring an ad in a women's business publication showing two women caught in the rain under one particular brand of umbrella, each with their hand holding the same umbrella together as they laugh and walk down a busy street, does not necessarily imagine they are supposed to be straight friends on their way to work or out to do some shopping.

For instance, each woman judges for herself what actually appeals to her sense of individuality, femininity, and community involvement when she looks at a piece of advertising. Still, there's a lot wrapped up in the visual communication of advertising and all the lines really blur when "same-sex sex appeal" becomes part of the picture—whether it was intended to be there or not.

Marketers who are not asking themselves these questions about the creative development within their advertising campaigns (and making informed decisions based on proper research) are probably costing their companies an indeterminable amount of money in what could otherwise be increased sales volume.

Consider the mixed emotions that some gay men feel when their eyes glance at the Marlboro Man cigarette billboards (which are often placed in the most conspicuous of gay male neighborhoods, yet the tobacco industry has never been a political friend of gay people). The robust, red-cotton-shirted man on the white horse, a stock (largely heterosexual) American role model for strength, ruggedness, and solid western tradition, becomes everything from a symbol of anger to divine comedy to exhausted sexual fantasy—especially for gay nonsmokers: a middle-aged man with a nicotine habit on a horse in the middle of nowhere trying to look straight?

Even Doublemint gum commercials tend to wax ludicrously campy in the eyes of some gay and lesbian consumers—the smiles, the hugging and laughing, the tongues, the rolling of the eyes— even the writing is an absolute riot. Consider the sing-songy lyrics: "double your pleasure, double your fun."

Sound too esoteric? Consider some of the advertising that appeared routinely in fashion magazines all through the 1970s and 1980s. Groups of men were often seen walking abreast, together or separately. There was nothing to suggest they were married, or even heterosexual. The ads were constructed in such a way that gay men could transpose themselves into the pictures, imagining that they were the intended target. The models were often photographed in neighborhoods that looked like places gay men lived or would travel to. The men were rarely touching, of course, but the line of demarcation was always played as close to the edge as possible. Occasionally, a token woman would be included. But same-sex affection was always hinted at with an eroticization not of the male body, but of the "sophisticated male look." Eventually, some men began to be described as looking "GQ"—a potential code word and clear radar detection device in gay culture.

If all this unintended sexual cross-pollination of consumer imagery sounds like a complicated dilemma for contemporary marketers and advertisers hoping to break into gay and lesbian market segments, it is . . . but it doesn't have to be an insurmountable one. Differing products must simply be dealt with based on geography and a sense of what can be pushed to the proper limits and what must be left alone. Strategically, the questions must still be asked:

- Does your company have gay and lesbian customers?
- Are you strengthening their loyalty to your products?
- What is your company's written policy regarding sexual orientation?
- Has anyone ever conducted gay market research?
- Has there been any history of insulting or neglecting gay and lesbian consumers by competitors?
- Can this be used to advantage?
- Is there a plan to ensure that a company does not make the same mistakes that its predecessors or competitors have already made?
- Is the company really ready and dedicated to growing its customer base by entering a given gay or lesbian market segment?
- Is your company currently sending mixed messages about gay and lesbian issues in its advertising?
- Are you sending any message? The wrong message?
- What is your message to gay and lesbian consumers?

If you consider the entire realm of images that modern cable television offers—live courtroom battles, child custody fights, murder follow-ups and ambulance rides, hundred-dollar juicers and miracle mops, *Hard Copy* re-runs, the (heterosexual) soft-porn channels, variations on the Thigh Master, Cher-touted hair care products that "really aren't sticky," all on par with "deadbeat dads who stalk the neighborhood" or "Monica Lewinsky finally talks on the next *Oprah*"—it's not hard to see why something as basic as targeting gay consumers is no longer seen as controversial.

Still, a company should know what it is doing.

PUTTING FIRST THINGS FIRST

To effectively understand, develop, and market products and services to gay and lesbian consumers today requires an acceptance and intellectual empathy for the stark division of visual images in modern life between heterosexual culture and what has been stereotypically touted and visually exemplified on the evening news as "the gay lifestyle" (usually old shelf footage of two young gay men walking hand in hand out of a bar onto the street of some assumed gay ghetto).

It also requires that business leaders be mindful of the way gay and lesbian citizens are treated by the American justice system, the police departments, the medical community, and the education system. Competent marketers must have a firm grasp of the general political issues and the divergent perceptions between gay and lesbian consumers' view of the world around them and those of heterosexuals if they are to ever successfully forge new ground in the wide spectrum of gay and lesbian market segments.

The shrewdest of America's business leaders who genuinely want to embrace the profits that come from doing business with gay and lesbian consumers must be willing to allow the pioneering information contained in this book, trade magazines, and other relevant sources to be burned into their consciousness if they are to understand the context within which the American gay consumer exists. Specific data and research in this particular area is discussed more in Chapter 4.

GAY IS GOOD—BIG IS NOT

Americans bore easily when it comes to the media's handling of an entire host of issues. And it is no wonder. All our major population centers have more than a hundred television channels of what, many often complain, amounts to nothing. Yet at any given moment, everything is available. The channel surfing continues.

We have it all. Test balloons on a myriad of issues are floated through the media daily by everyone from the Justice Department and the White House to the Home Shopping Channel and municipal governments. Senate, congressional, and presidential announcements are molded, timed, and delivered with simultaneous monitoring (which we hear later as a poll). And there is always a "pullback" position in case the numbers don't pan out as hoped.

Indeed, more and more Americans have a sneaking suspicion that what is often passing for news these days is simply "information product" filtered through public relations firms. They are not far from the mark. I am told by public relations people that publicists often have shouting matches with columnists and talk show coordinators over who's getting "the exclusive."

We are lost in an endless barrage of commercial messaging designed to develop us into, or keep us part of, a particular market share. It all boils down to competition. And of course, money—which is one of the main reasons why gay and lesbian visibility has appeared so quickly in the American commercial spectrum, and why it has also been so quickly embraced as a market dynamic.

It is the very impact of the telecommunication explosion—in concert with shrewd gay and lesbian political activism—that has solidly awakened America to a host of issues surrounding not only gays and lesbians but heterosexuals as well: blatant discrimination, physical and emotional abuse of men and women in the armed services, AIDS, breast cancer, child abuse, religious extremism, and the ongoing health care crisis.

A *Time*/CNN News poll found that, of those questioned, 62 percent of Americans favor the passage of equal rights laws to protect gays and lesbians against job discrimination. Yet 65 percent of those same Americans also indicated that too much attention was being paid to homosexual rights.[3]

The general feeling seems to be that we did the gays in the military thing. We watched the gays in Washington thing. We saw the Gay Games thing. We saw Ellen come out. We watched her go away. As a television viewing nation we've simply become bored with the issues surrounding the equal rights process for gay and lesbian Americans. Interestingly enough, we're certainly not bored with gay and lesbian culture when it comes to investigating the same issues through entertainment venues, as witnessed by the growing number of television shows and motion pictures being released over the last few years that deal with gay and lesbian characters and social concerns.

Heterosexual Americans may be bored with equal rights for lesbians and gay men, but they are fascinated with same-sex drama and intrigue. Greg Louganis's *Breaking the Surface* jumped to number one on *The New York Times* best-seller list in less than three weeks after its release. We couldn't get enough of the scandal surrounding Michael Jackson's alleged sleeping arrangements with young boys and what that might say about his "real" sex life. We delighted in the naughtiness of George Michael's arrest in a Beverly Hills rest room. And the afternoon talk shows continue to mesmerize us with every variation on gaydom imaginable. A mere decade ago, gay and lesbian visibility was largely segregated to a select few urban zip codes known as gay ghettos.

Those days are over.

COMMUNICATING SENSITIVITY

Marketing any consumer product today is tough enough. Just getting slightly ahead or making a product perform enough to maintain its market share requires tenacious writers and art directors as well as hyperinformed, shrewd-thinking account people working in concert to create hard-hitting multilevel advertising promotions and public relations campaigns.

Account people complain about the fine line they have to walk between making their clients feel comfortable with their creative team's work and the superiors they report to versus what is actually needed to deliver the numbers that will register as increased sales in the final analysis and when the agency's contract comes up for review.

Advertising creative people talk about the insanity, the pressure, and the deviousness with which a product's quality is touted, misrepresented or, occasionally, outright lied about as it is shoved into the commercial limelight of mass consumption with its frequent-flyer miles, rewards, rebates, replays, and loyalty programs. Any strategy will be tried to sell a product, push an agenda, communicate an idea, disenfranchise an institution, defame an opponent, or win an election.

Our modern commercial institutions have used in-your-face visibility, overly sexualized imagery, planted rumors, and disinformation combined with an offensive level of backroom politics and lust for profit to deliver or fumble everything from the success of the Ford Taurus to the bungled attempt to change the recipe of Coca-Cola.

America is now a commercialized Orwellian jungle sweating out programs, products, and images one by one into the line of fire for a chance at the center stage in the amphitheater of mass consumerism. In television news media, content is now secondary to the sensationalized visual imagery and the packaging of shock value—which is why news is no longer news but a product produced and spun by "media companies" (all of which—including major newspapers—are now owned by one of twenty-three multinational corporations).[4] Today, hype and controversy have become the norm itself and gay consumers are especially sensitive to it. Former *Advocate* associate publisher Stephanie Blackwood agrees, stating that marketers should bear in mind that "lesbians in America have been conditioned based on twenty-five years of the women's movement."

What marketers need to understand is that gay and lesbian consumers are much more cynical when it comes to the potential dangers and implications of our overly commercialized modern society. This is because it is a society that has largely excluded them, forcing them to constantly reevaluate themselves and their relationship to the images at hand. Not all gay and lesbian consumers are able to articulate these feelings, but they know it intuitively and indicate such feelings in focus groups and national polls.

To communicate with gay and lesbian consumers is to reinvent sensitivity—to reengineer "realness" by communicating and mirroring the best in gay and lesbian culture as it is and can be—not as it has been assumed and stereotyped.

UNDERSTANDING THE INFLUENCE
OF THE GAY MALE AESTHETIC

Until the late 1970s, the use of sex to sell a product stopped abruptly at the depiction of same-sex affection beyond the platonic. Such depictions were a basic no-no—especially in the depiction of men's needs and desires. Women were allowed to be seen holding, touching, hugging, even adoring each other. The rules of heterosexual behavior have always decreed such behavior as the rightful domain of being "feminine," being "passive," being ladylike. Any image that could be argued to be too undeniably "homosexually suggestive" (of men or women) was quietly accepted to be the road "safely not taken."

However, with the emergence of code came endless commercialized closetry and lots of eroticization of the male body—something that was just never done before, but continues to grow directly out of gay male cultural, political, and aesthetic constructionism. With regard to men and the domain of the masculine, subtly hinting at bisexuality was quietly permissible so long as there was a level of deniability in the creative execution—usually the token placement of a single woman.

Prior to the 1970s, the woman's body was eroticized. Men generally did not appear in advertising, on television, or in film in any aggressively focused way that accentuated their bodies. That was the domain of the female flesh. Men appeared in bathing suits or with their shirts off in a love scene—that was about it. Men were sexualized by whether they had that distinguished touch of gray in their hair, if they had money, if they were youthful, gentlemanly, or great businessmen. Men were sexual if they were single, and they were sexy if they were married but they were never objectified as sexual objects the way women were.

Much has changed. Today there is so much mixed messaging and outright eroticizing of both sexes in any number of combinations that there's very little line to cross any more when it comes to sexuality, only varying degrees of creative boundary based on industry progressiveness, media buying, and perceived visual tolerances in relation to geography and demographics. The eroticization of the male body is now as much required in the selling of products as the pursuit of the female breast. And with all this new sexual focus on men is finally coming a sense of sanity and experimentation toward gay and lesbian marketing.

With each passing month, more and more companies are willing to explore and depict the heretofore forbidden realm of romantic, same-sex attraction in the marketing of products. And it's most apparent in their modern treatment and eroticization of the male form—something that has actually helped liberate heterosexual men. Today more businesses are becoming familiar with testing and launching marketing campaigns that contain intentionally suggestive gay or lesbian subject matter with increasing degrees of verisimilitude.

In New York City, a Hugo Boss advertising campaign on public transit buses shows three men in a picture. Two are standing close to each other, with one looking over his shoulder to the third gentleman, who is standing alone. The gentleman standing alone seems to be reacting to the two standing together. Is he supposed to be jealous? Perplexed? Wondering about the relationship of the two men standing together? Or is he supposed to be the guy "all alone" who needs to buy Hugo Boss to be a part of some particular group? Any combination is possible depending on the perspective of the consumer.

Ambiguous and somewhat coded? Yes. Progressive advertising? Certainly. Because it requires men, gay or straight, to ponder the image's intended message. The result is still the same: Hugo Boss on the brain of male consumers regardless of sexual orientation.

Sensitive and informed fashion, media, and advertising professionals understand these relationships and have also begun using them to increase the visibility of lesbians. Along the way a kind of pansexual sensitivity emerged. Calvin Klein's new cologne called One is a perfect example of this new blurring of boundaries.

CHANGING TIMES
FOR THE GAY AND LESBIAN
CONSUMER, EMPLOYEE, AND INVESTOR

Things are happening where gay and lesbian consumers make purchasing and investing decisions. They are also happening where they earn their living.

Through the systematic rewriting of employment policy statements in thousands of companies nationwide, gays and lesbians are actually effecting change on a fundamental level in American society. Insurance policy and employee benefit packages at major corporations are also being rewritten. And they are increasingly affecting the stakes by which corporations attract and keep America's most educated, talented, and productive workers—both gay and straight. Such policies are also becoming important in the decisions that institutional—as well as individual—investors make regarding company stock purchases.

It should not strike anyone as surprising that some of America's most progressive companies, with the best track records on gay and lesbian workplace issues, are also some of the most up-and-coming forces in the marketing of their products to gay and lesbian consumers—many of whom consider such information when making investments.

For readers who are new to the equal rights movement for gay and lesbian citizens, or its relationship to the overall American economy, three strategic points need to be understood:

- Media has misrepresented the character and demographics of American gay and lesbian culture
- Gay Americans feel all the same emotions about life, God, and country as straight Americans
- Gay and lesbian culture in the Western world has undergone more change in the past fifteen years than at any time in recorded history

All the varying social issues and economic challenges that are faced daily by heterosexual Americans—whether as citizens, parents, consumers, teenagers, veterans, or employees—also exist in varying degrees for lesbians and gay men in every city, town, and rural community in America.

All the phobias, ignorance, and tensions relating to race, religion, status, income, class, and education also apply in varying degrees to the lives of gays and lesbians—including the historical compulsion to render women of all backgrounds essentially invisible.[5]

Although gay and lesbian visibility is higher today than it has ever been in the modern world, it must be readily accepted that vast numbers of bisexuals, lesbians, and gay men have always been working in the American economy since the founding of the republic—indeed in the history of humankind.

Recognizing oneself as gay, lesbian, or bisexual is (in varying degrees) a spiritual, emotional, physical, political, and (now) economic "identity" in exactly the same visceral way that being straight is an "identity." One is one's sexuality; something that is a complex conglomeration of an individual's spiritual and emotional essence.

The politics and understanding of identity and its relationship to freedom and expression are constantly evolving. Consider the following passage:

> ... homosexuals are discarding their furtive ways and openly admitting, even flaunting, their deviation. Homosexuals have their own drinking places, their special assignation streets, even their own organizations. And for every obvious homosexual, there are probably nine nearly impossible to detect.[6]

This was the lead paragraph in a *Life* magazine article just thirty years ago. When this passage is compared to the Nut 'n' Honey cereal commercials, one can see how little things appeared to change between the early 1960s and the late 1980s.

All through those years, the myth perpetuated to heterosexual Americans was that gays and lesbians were immoral and criminal by using the word "deviant," or psychologically sick by characterizing them as being prissy degenerates at the root of a "social disorder." Many references refused to acknowledge that women could also be gay, because that was an equally radical notion that would have required that the word "lesbian" be printed in a national publication.

A second article on the psychology of homosexuality in the same issue of *Life*, stated that "A bad case of acne, a stammer, or unusual shyness may make a boy feel so unwanted in the world of boy-meets-girl that he quickly embraces the other world." The article included a parenthetical aside stating that "many a homosexual affair . . . is an alliance between two men who both consider themselves 'social cripples'."[7]

It is against this historical perspective of gay and lesbian Americans in the media that gay and lesbian individuals started their own newspapers, their own political groups and, essentially, their own culture. By 1975, the national gay and lesbian community was galloping full steam ahead toward becoming an important new marketplace.

The beginning of this phenomenon was certainly elusive but solid—so solid, in fact, that motion picture producers, liquor distributors, boutiques, and theatrical performance revues were beginning to discreetly advertise to gays and lesbians, and word of this evolution began to hit the mainstream as it was calmly documented in *The Wall Street Journal* as early as 1975.[8]

Yet outside of some brief mentions in trade articles (and an infuriating but motivating rallying call to antigay activism provided by Anita Bryant), few noticed that gay and lesbian culture was becoming more than a fringe political movement; few would have even believed that it was in fact on its way to becoming one of the most important socioeconomic forces the twentieth century would see.

But gays and lesbians saw it everywhere. And much of the country danced right alongside them, not realizing that a new consumer revolution was gearing up. Gloria Gaynor belted it out loud and clear and made it stick: "Never Can Say Goodbye" stayed on the *Billboard* Top 40 for ten weeks. All of America simply "danced to the beat of the disco" and the sound of Village People's rallying tribal call: "Macho, macho man; I've got to be a macho man," which belted out of radios ad nauseam.

Gay and lesbian culture was seeping into the mainstream marketplace. It was evident in the way gay writer Jerry Blatt influenced Bette Midler and the cult of her gay and lesbian following (eventually extended to Middle America with the help of Walt Disney Studios). It was evident in the following that the Pointer Sisters were developing. Rock music stars dripped with androgyny. David Bowie, Janis Ian, the Rolling Stones, the British music invasion, Rock Hudson, Levi's button-fly jeans, the women's music movement—it all had affectionate same-sex overtones that woke up gays and lesbians throughout the country.

But that was before anyone had been diagnosed.

COMMUNICATING LEGITIMACY
IN AN AGE OF GRIEF

By the early 1980s, the AIDS epidemic had crystallized and magnified nearly every issue that gay and lesbian citizens had been confronting throughout American history. AIDS, in effect, mainstreamed gay and lesbian visibility in the United States. It exponentially increased gay and lesbian political coverage in both national and local media. In time, the media became more levelheaded in its coverage of gay and lesbians, but with the increased visibility came a nearly proportional increase in violence against gays and lesbians nationwide. A domino effect began.

Political rhetoric heated up on Capitol Hill in Washington and in state legislatures across the country. Religious groups began using the power of the religious broadcasting networks to disseminate falsehoods and politically self-serving information about morality, the wrath of God, and the breakdown of the family (something that was going on in the nineteenth century as well).

Radical health officials began arguing for quarantines; political extremists called for tattooing of people testing HIV positive.

For many in the American gay and lesbian community, being out and visible became literally tantamount to staying alive. For others, staying quiet seemed safer.

Many gay and lesbian citizens became terrified, even fearful that the country was drifting toward fascism. Indeed, for a time, it appeared that the McCarthy Era was returning. And at the time, Ronald Reagan looked no more a friend to gays and lesbians than Eisenhower turned out to be in 1950s.

It is under these conditions that gay and lesbian activism, visibility, and consumerism erupted with a vengeance unseen since Stonewall. We watched CNN as ACT UP demonstrators disrupted business at the Wall Street stock exchange in an eleventh-hour attempt to wake people up about the hypocrisy in the health care industry and how big business was price-gouging the dying.

We watched AIDS activists march into St. Patrick's Cathedral in New York City, disrupting Mass, and demanding to know why American taxpayer money was going to hospitals run by the Catholic Church—an institution that refuses to acknowledge the importance of educating people about condom usage to prevent the spread of HIV, the virus that causes AIDS.

In 1990, a courageous new gay and lesbian magazine called *Outweek* was thrust onto national newsstands. It dared to call Madison Avenue's bluff by removing all its sexually oriented advertising and then reminded wholesalers across the country that they would be in violation of restraint of trade legislation if they refused to place the publication in suburban retail outlets.

Outweek printed the same kind of intimate journalism and gossip about people's lives that Ann Landers, Liz Smith, and Rona Barrett had discussed about heterosexuals for years. It also printed the truth about Covenant House in New York City and Malcom Forbes's attraction to young men, and exposed the carefully hidden secrets behind Washington and Hollywood's hypocrisy, lies, and double standards.

None of these developments served to make the business world comfortable with advertising to gay and lesbian consumers. Consequently, for a few years, it didn't really matter how much statistical information was being presented by gay and lesbian political leaders, market authorities, and newspaper publishers; corporations were simply not ready to jump into the gay and lesbian marketplace because it looked to be a sure public relations fiasco.

In retrospect however, it now appears that *Outweek* and other groups' amplification of gay, lesbian, and AIDS activism prompted a significant nationwide shift in thinking. Suddenly new financial contributions began flowing into the nation's AIDS organizations from once-closeted public figures. New films and television programs came out of Hollywood with more accurate portrayals of gay and lesbian people. AIDS and human rights concerns began seeping into nighttime television dramas.

More domestic partnership task forces cropped up at large corporations and small businesses around the country, allowing more gay and lesbian employees to petition for the same spousal benefits that their heterosexual co-workers enjoyed. The 1990s saw more celebrities, actors, politicians, and musicians coming out publicly as gays and lesbians, activists and modern revolutionaries in true Jeffersonian style, than in all the previous decades of the twentieth century put together.

Finally, in concert with America's contemporary communication explosion, the thirst for a sound bite, and a new twist on the old, the country woke up from its traditional perspective about human sexuality. It had stumbled upon the voices of gay and lesbian Americans because there was an actual increase in the amount of coverage on the very issues that were of concern to them.

Ironically, with all the gay-bashing that occurred at the 1994 Republican National Convention in Houston, Texas, many issues of concern to gay, lesbian, and bisexual Americans were actually moved all the more rapidly to the fore of American consciousness. In the mid-1980s, AIDS indirectly brought more attention to lesbian mothers and gay fathers. The investigations into the transgendered community were among the first great afternoon talk show subjects because they upped the ante on sexual voyeurism in the media—a consistent and dynamic theme in television entertainment, one that did for afternoon ratings what violence apparently can do for evening ratings.

But over time, those subjects become commonplace discussion. By the 1990s, the talk shows were beginning to explore outing, gay and lesbian palimony, discrimination in the armed services, and the sinister corporate behavior of the insurance industry and the constrictions it was placing on gay and lesbian families.

Against all the cable television competition and hype, there was a steady stream of programming about gay and lesbian Americans— that, in fact, they are not treated equally by their government, and lose their jobs, their children, their health insurance—some, their very lives. Hype had given way to a degree of reality.

On a scale unprecedented, heterosexual American society began experiencing and understanding through media what gays and lesbians experienced in the Harlem Renaissance and the flourishing of bohemianism early in the century: a more collective and mirrored self-awareness of the nation's diverse sexual makeup. The growth and legitimacy of gay and lesbian culture in America had at long last become utterly unavoidable. Newsrooms couldn't deny the growing size of the marches around the country.

The Gay and Lesbian Alliance Against Defamation began forming chapters in every major city. Queer Nation was born. The Lesbian Avengers came into being.

The public was astonished (but later enchanted) by the sheer size and friendliness of gay and lesbian freedom day parades and the shrewd effectiveness and ability of activists to capture international television cameras and raise public consciousness on a number of issues—almost on a daily basis. The AIDS crisis forced the country to acknowledge even further the extent to which gay and lesbian culture existed, and that tens of thousands were now dying in the epidemic.

Today there is a new era of candor about gay culture in America. It is a candor that is allowing business to begin listening to the logic of America's gay and lesbian newspaper publishers, advertising sales executives, direct marketers, and event coordinators.

In midsized American cities, the increase of visibility of gays and lesbians has often become directly proportional to the degree of intolerance displayed by local-area politicians—especially when the intolerance represents political strategy at the expense of gays and lesbians, rather than voting constituency.

This dynamic, for instance, was recently apparent in Indianapolis, Indiana, when the state legislature temporarily decided against including the words "sexual orientation" in an intensely debated hate crimes bill. At the time, the legislature refused to protect its gay and lesbian citizens (claiming it would be legitimizing a "lifestyle"). This social bigotry brought out more gay and lesbian activists across Indiana than ever before, fueling a debate over sexual politics unlike any Indiana had ever seen. Gay and lesbian issues began filling the radio airwaves and nightly newscasts of Indiana's television screens. The *Indianapolis Star and News* began regularly assessing sexual politics on its editorial page, placing a variety of issues of gay and lesbian emancipation, civil rights, and individual liberty protections on the front burner of Indiana politics.

For the first time, gay and lesbian Hoosiers were prime-time news. A media item. A new local-area commodity sandwiched between General Motors car commercials, Pacer basketball scores, and agricultural reports.

But it didn't stop there. Gay and lesbian issues were beginning to be discussed in the workplace with a greater degree of intensity. Gay and lesbian Hoosiers began rereading their employee benefits manuals at work, looking for the words "sexual orientation" in their companies' hiring and employment practices.

And when gay pride season came around in June, more people attended their local celebrations than ever before in the state's history. And it was not just gays and lesbians in attendance. They brought their children, friends, and parents, most of whom vote, buy products, and will no doubt now consider an elected official's position on gay and lesbian issues of liberty and civil rights.

That event alone (Indiana's first public gay and lesbian celebration, begun only four years earlier) required street vending permits for over forty businesses hoping to attract gay and lesbian consumers, and most of all, it set a pioneering, visible precedence of free enterprise and respect for everyone in the middle of America's heartland for years to come.

Consequently, politics has shown just how responsive businesses, gay and lesbian consumers, and their families and friends can be in cities as conservative as Indianapolis when it comes to individual rights. It shows that in cities large and small, marketing relationships are becoming inextricably tied to gay and lesbian visibility and respect for individuality.

In New York City, this dynamic directly affected the turnout for the twenty-fifth anniversary of the Stonewall Riots, which coincided with the Gay Games IV and Cultural Festival. City controller Alan Hevisi conservatively estimated that the 1994 Gay Games IV brought well over 400 million dollars into the New York City area economy. And that is not counting the hundreds of thousands of dollars racked up by airlines and travel agencies around the world.

At the same time, AT&T launched its first direct marketing campaign aimed specifically at thousands of known gay and lesbian households in all fifty states, implicitly expressing their support for the importance of gay and lesbian political issues, and simultaneously urging them to switch their long-distance service to AT&T.

That same month, Perrier and Calistoga bottled water began running advertisements in gay and lesbian papers and magazines across the United States. Miller Beer joined with AT&T and Continental Airlines in sponsoring the Gay Games, which crescendoed with a sellout crowd in Yankee Stadium with performances by Patti LaBelle and a march that ended in Central Park the following day with a performance by Liza Minnelli.

Clearly, gay and lesbian pride celebrations each June create a steady and important rhythm around which gay activists, gay consumers, and gay-friendly companies can rally. They also serve to keep a sense of visibility and civic responsibility instilled in younger gay and lesbian groups as the national media slowly learns how to cover, interpret, and report gay and lesbian news in its proper context without bias and without being afraid to be critical in its observations.

Business has come to understand that gay and lesbian consumerism is not a flash in the pan but an evolving and stable, long-term development in modern marketing.

What business must now accept is that the media has ironically fallen prey to its own infatuation with the gay market story—which has resulted in more misrepresentation and harsh statistical stereotyping about gay and lesbian affluence. This has been fueled by a lack of responsibility on behalf of some gay-owned research firms and publishers that have, at times, sought to portray out-of-context information about gay and lesbian magazine readers as being representative of the overall gay and lesbian population. This has led to the development of more myths about gay and lesbian Americans—that they are all dual-income households with no children and a higher-than-average disposable income, allowing them to take worldwide vacations and drink premium Scotch whiskies while listening to Vivaldi. Which, of course, is not true.

What is true is that a favorable portion of some dual earning, urban gay male baby boomer households do appear to have an arguably above-average disposable income. But the fiction common around most television and newspaper newsrooms about the vast majority of gay and lesbian Americans and their money is simply misguided, sloppily researched, and improperly characterized.

The American media's ongoing carelessness in reporting gay and lesbian economic news has led to an inexcusable level of misinformation being picked up and used by radical right-wing extremists as an argument to roll back gay and lesbian equal rights gains at many municipal levels (as if affluence was a reason to deny an American his or her rights).

Unfortunately for marketers, much of the economic research prior to 1993 on income and parenthood among the majority of gays and lesbians is not really useful in understanding them as a national group. In fact, according to the research conducted exclusively for this book by Yankelovich Partners, much of it appears to be astonishingly inaccurate or based on methods that no industry trade publication would dare report if it were used to explain anything about heterosexual consumers as a national population. This is why, in the next chapter, we will place a big magnifying glass on all the studies worth looking at, what they say, and what they don't say—and how business can make better, more useful sense of it all.

Chapter 3

Will the Real Gay Consumers
Please Stand Up?

*American business must realize that while the shareholders
always come first, the care and feeding of their customer is a
close second.*

Harvey Milk

Have you ever heard of the lucrative heterosexual market? Probably not. A heterosexual market, per se, has never really existed in marketing language. Until recently, nearly all consumer marketing was nothing but heterosexual. It was built around growth of the nuclear family, housing starts, savings for the kid's college tuition, and so on.

It wasn't until the visibility and growth of the gay and lesbian political, cultural, and consumer revolution came about that any other kind of consumer buying pattern was even considered by marketers. Even as segmentation became more the norm, marketing was really aimed toward "segments of heterosexuals"—consumers we could identify in more focused ways, but who were just taken for granted as being straight.

Today, leading companies are applying the science of segmentation in a way that includes gay and lesbian consumers as well as heterosexuals. But our understanding and the strategies we employ in our pursuit of gay and lesbian consumers must be applied in the same segmented ways that have been applied to heterosexuals. In reality, gay and lesbian market segments exist in much the same way that heterosexual market segments exist. Determining the size and breakdown of each of those gay and lesbian consumer segments requires the same kind of approach that has been used to determine the demographics, human values, needs, wants, fears, and dreams in varying segments of what were once assumed to be all straight consumers.

So, in determining the demographics and psychographics of the modern consumer marketplace, our focus must begin to include sexual identity as part of the overall marketing strategy, and our focus on gay and lesbian consumers, per se, must be of a segmented, targetable nature as well.

Soon, more consumer market segmentation analysis will have to take into account the degree to which product and service sales include gay and lesbian buying patterns—if companies want to keep the gay and lesbian consumers they have, or want to attract new consumers in the future.

ELEVATING THE DISCUSSION AND THE SCIENCE

Without digressing into the politics of numbers, let us remember that any number cited as a measure of a gay or lesbian population in the United States is only as good as the methodology used to arrive at it.

To begin to quantify the potential gay and lesbian marketplace, I have compiled quick overviews of all the relevant studies of gay and lesbian sexuality conducted in this century. Most of the studies have sought to understand gay and lesbian sexuality and how that sexuality exists within the larger heterosexual majority. But first, some basic questions must be addressed regarding how these studies were conducted and what they say about gay and lesbian consumers in America.

Was convenience or random sampling used to obtain the participants? Are the results generalizable or scientifically applicable to the overall population—therefore representative and logically supportive of the conclusions drawn? Were questionnaires, interviews, and observations conducted face to face? Were written documents and questionnaires presented in a confidential setting or an anonymous setting? (There is a difference.)

Recently, more and more studies have been cited as the latest source for determining the numbers of gay men and lesbians in the

United States. However, upon closer scrutiny, most of the studies cited had merely investigated varying degrees of sexual behavior in the human species; they did not conclude that the individual saw himself or herself as "being" gay or lesbian. Nor did those studies arrive at conclusions based on behavior that would help marketers consider such individuals as prospective customers in a targeted gay- or lesbian-oriented advertising campaign.

Researching and analyzing sexual behavior and sexual orientation and how they affect an individual's sense of sexual identity is tough work. It requires highly sophisticated methodology, competent scientists, rock-solid funding, and political proficiency in academic circles.

When we apply these dynamics to the science of consumer behavior, and then attempt to understand their relationships to our increasingly segmented and globally interactive marketplace, we are faced with a number of complex problems that begin to appear insurmountable. A mere study of sexual behavior will not answer the questions today's businesspeople want answered about gay and lesbian people as consumers.

All of these problems do not mean, however, that economists, psychologists, political pollsters, and market researchers are incapable of coming up with a reasonably acceptable estimate of the likely size of the American gay and lesbian population. Nor does it mean that we can't determine how varying groups of gay and lesbian consumers think, shop, save, and spend their money differently from heterosexual consumers.

Such numbers and meaningful, more reliable data do exist, and depending on who you listen to and hold accountable, they indeed have significant relevance to understanding the art and science of gay and lesbian consumer economics. But a delineation between studies and what they actually represent must be addressed.

This takes us to the Yankelovich Partners, Yankelovich MONITOR Gay and Lesbian Perspective—the most important research conducted on gay and lesbian consumers to date. The Yankelovich MONITOR research on gay and lesbian Americans is truly unlike any other study in the United States because it sought to understand gay and lesbian consumer thinking and behavior as opposed to sexual behavior and conditioning. This research accurately and comprehensively

addresses the questions business wants answered about gay and lesbian demographics and psychographics in relation to the economics
of the population as a whole, based on random sampling and
weighted against U.S. Census data.

But before briefly summarizing the various studies and then
making my case for some general conclusions in relationship to
Yankelovich MONITOR findings, I'd like to indulge in a couple of
reminders regarding the basics of sexually oriented research, and
how the media's somewhat casual use of sexually oriented language
has diluted the public's understanding of the facts. The first pertains
to sex and and the second pertains to identity and who we are
talking about when we say "the gay and lesbian marketplace."

Plenty of studies have attempted to determine the number of
people, by sex, in the human species who have ever had a homosexual experience. But such studies are of relatively little use in determining the number of American consumers who see themselves as
gay or lesbian—and who are therefore likely to respond to the
commercial environment in a way that is of interest to marketers.

The overall number of targetable gay and lesbian market segments,
and the sum of prospective consumers that that number represents, is
not at all equal to some scientific estimate of the number of people in
the human species who have ever had a romantic or sexual experience
with a member of the same sex.

Simply put: the incidence of homosexual behavior in the population is not proportional to the number of gay and lesbian consumers
that can be targeted by a company, political party, or marketing
study group. For marketers, it really does not matter how many
people are having, are likely to have, or have at some time had, a
sexual experience with a member of the same sex. Sexual behavior
alone is not a barometer of whether or not an individual can be
considered part of any prospective consumer cohort.

Still, a marketer must obviously be able to determine where the
prospective customers are. Therefore, what really matters is being
able to determine the total number of individuals who self-identify as
being gay or lesbian within any given geographic area. But, they
must be given a scientifically fair and equal opportunity to do so.

The concept of self-identity remains as the most important dynamic that must first be addressed and considered before relying on

any data claiming to represent the size of gay and lesbian consumer populations anywhere. If we can't at least determine who is identifiable, then how can we determine who to target?

STAYING MINDFUL OF STATISTICAL GAMES

Now a brisk reminder about shortcomings in sexual research. The most common involve the manner in which individuals are obtained for the research—including the way in which they are questioned.

Many sexually oriented studies arrive at conclusions based on "convenience sampling," meaning that participants are obtained through institutions, government offices, schools, or public health clinics. In some cases they are approached in shopping malls, public events, and transportation terminals and then paid to participate. The Kinsey research from the early part of the twentieth century has been cited for this particular shortcoming because some of his critics believed that too many of his participants came from medical institutions, prisons, and schools and therefore gave a biased view of sexuality (particularly with regard to homosexuality in men).

When convenience samples are used in sexually oriented research, the probability that the conclusions can be projected to the national population becomes highly questionable.

The most reliable research (in terms of relevance to the overall population) needs to be based on what is often referred to as "random probability"—meaning that participants in the survey have been selected in a scientifically hygienic way, ensuring that their responses will be reasonably representative of the general population with regard to geography, race, ethnicity, religion, education, culture bias, etc. The Yankelovich MONITOR's Gay and Lesbian Perspective meets this rigid requirement.[1]

HOW WE GOT TO WHERE WE ARE

During the 1980s, many advertising-starved gay and lesbian news publications across the United States set out to identify, study, and publish information highlighting their readers' income, affluence, and education.

Since newspaper and magazine readers (in fact, readers in general) tend to be more educated and have a higher disposable income than those who don't subscribe to periodicals, a new stereotype began brewing about the wealth of gay Americans. This notion came about largely because the statistics that were getting media coverage were based on biased information—that of newspaper readerships rather than scientifically researched income levels generalizable to the overall self-identified gay and lesbian population.

In actuality, the majority of lesbians and gay men in the United States earn slightly less than heterosexuals. This fact was demonstrated in a recent study conducted by economist Lee Badgett of the University of Maryland.[2] Badgett's recent findings substantially parallel research conducted by Yankelovich Partners, which also found that self-identified gay and lesbian Americans, in fact, do not earn more than heterosexuals (see Table 3.1).

The wealthiest segment of gay and lesbian Americans is restricted to a minority of older, dual-income, white male households in the country's largest urban areas, which actually represents only a fraction of the overall gay and lesbian population. Since men tend to earn more than women, it is only natural that this minority of gay

TABLE 3.1. 1994 Yankelovich MONITOR's Gay and Lesbian Perspective

	Gay/Lesbian %	Heterosexual %
Personal Income:		
Under $25K	85	78
$25K-$49,999	12	19
$50K-$99,999	2	3
$100K+	1	*
Household Income:		
Under $25K	44	38
$25K-$49,999	39	39
$50K-$99,999	14	20
$100K+	3	3
Mean Personal Income (000)	$16.9	$17.6
Mean Household Income (000)	$35.8	$36.7
Mean Household Size	2.89	3.01

*Less than 0.5%.

Americans would have a higher household income than most heterosexuals because of women's decreased earning power in comparison to men.

Unfortunately, the idea that gay and lesbian Americans are more affluent is the impression that most Americans were left with after the media explosion discovered gay and lesbian consumerism. To a certain extent, the misconception that gays and lesbians have more money than heterosexuals actually awakened many in business to the nature of gay and lesbian market segments—even though the shattering of the myth of more widespread affluence was somewhat of a letdown in the short term for pioneering marketers.

Still, the end result has been that gay and lesbian consumers are everywhere. Certainly nobody in marketing is disputing it, especially after the hundreds of thousands of people made their identities very clear by participating in the 1993 gay and lesbian national March on Washington, the 1994 Gay Games IV, and the twenty-fifth anniversary commemoration of the Stonewall Riots in New York City.

IDENTIFYING THE CONSUMERS THAT MATTER

In a middle-size American city of, say, two million residents, the difference between a study that claims ten percent of the population is gay or lesbian (200,000 people) versus two percent (40,000) is politically irrelevant. Individual rights are individual rights whether they're applied to two million, 200,000, 40,000, or four. In a marketing context, however, numbers and methodology become very relevant. Forty thousand potential consumers in a given geographic region is significantly different from 200,000.

Until the complete presentation of the Yankelovich MONITOR's Gay and Lesbian Perspective was made available in the first edition of this book, no widely published study in the history of market-oriented research has representatively examined the number of individuals in the United States who identify as gay, lesbian, or homosexual within the context of consumer behavior.

No doubt, some parallels may be found between separately existing research on sexual behavior of gays and lesbians and consumer behavior of the population as a whole, but these parallels are insufficient in determining the more sophisticated issues pertaining directly to gay and lesbian psychographics.

According to John Knoebel, vice president of *The Advocate,* some preliminary research was conducted by the Walker Struman research firm in 1968. It was probably the first media research firm to conduct any kind of professional study of gay and lesbian consumers in the United States through its groundbreaking study of the readership of *The Advocate,* then one of the few gay and lesbian publications in the United States (at the time its readership was almost exclusively male; the word "lesbian" did not appear on the cover of *The Advocate* until 1990).

The late Frank Vinci, a former advertising director with *The Advocate,* recalled the demand for Walker Struman's research and even remembered "other companies stealing the information" and using it to sell *The Advocate*'s gay and lesbian market to their potential advertisers.

Other than *The Advocate*'s early research, none of the previous studies of homosexuality conducted in this century were motivated by the need for consumer behavioral information; they were largely commissioned out of a need to know about sexual behavior exclusively or the degree to which such status should be interpreted and recognized in the evaluation of policy (as in the case of the Rand report on sexual orientation and U.S. military personnel policy).

As a general rule, research indicates that the larger population centers of the country are where the most self-identified gay and lesbian consumers are to be found. Table 3.2 shows how the percentages break down by population for those gay and lesbian individuals who identified themselves in the Yankelovich study.

Just looking at known gay and lesbian consumer markets based on population percentages is only a base point by which companies can begin targeting gay and lesbian consumers. In the long run, independently conducted research aimed at a company's current or developing gay and lesbian consumer base is the best way to develop a strategy for keeping those customers and learning how to go after the competition's customers as well. In general, marketers need to monitor and understand how their current gay and lesbian consumers' perceptions differ from those of straights.

TABLE 3.2. Distribution of Gay/Lesbian Population Among Metropolitan Area Sizes

	Total Population %	Gay/Lesbian %
Metropolitan area size:		
3 million +	19	27
1-3 million	27	34
500K-999,999	13	12
250K-499,999	10	8
100K-249,999	9	5
nonmetropolitan area	22	14
	100	100
All counties in 25 largest metros:	39	56

For instance, winter coats are not going to sell as briskly to gay or straight consumers in Southern California as they are in the northeastern part of the country. But a certain kind of coat by a particular manufacturer may do better with gay consumers in Manhattan versus gay consumers in Boston. Obviously, only localized research and follow-up sales tracking are going to shed light on such a question.

In addition, a point needs to be made regarding the visibility of self-identified gay and lesbian consumers—by region. Some areas might appear to be lacking a well-organized gay and lesbian political community, but that does not necessarily mean that there is a lack of gay and lesbian consumer prospects. Sometimes the quietest gay and lesbian communities make the best sales prospects—this is especially worth considering when launching direct mail campaigns in the South and Midwest.

Indeed, some of the country's midsized cities and communities have populated and very active gay and lesbian consumer economies, but comparatively tamer and less nationally recognized levels of political visibility—cities such as Dallas, Houston, Detroit, Indianapolis, and Seattle. Then there are the vacation areas such as Provincetown, Massachusetts; the Russian River area in Northern California; Austin, Texas; Hawaii; and Ft. Lauderdale, Miami, and Key West, Florida. All are excellent geographic areas worthy of consideration for target marketing campaigns, print advertising, and public relations efforts aimed at gay consumers.

THE POPULATION ESTIMATES
ON GAY AND LESBIAN AMERICANS

I have compiled Table 3.3 and Figure 3.1 extrapolating a sampling of various studies and the population estimates they arrived at for the total number of gay Americans by race, religion, and geography but in relationship to the 1990 census report. Table 3.3 illustrates in black and white just how divergent the range of conclusions really is when the numbers regarding what percentage of the population might be gay or lesbian are compared side by side and in relation to the population as a whole.

I've started with the single most verifiable number (the 1990 census) and compared that to the most liberal estimate (Kinsey 1948), to the most conservative (Guttmacher 1993), to the most representative of both sexes (Harris 1988 from the Rand Report), and to the most representative average of self-identified gay men and lesbians (Yankelovich MONITOR 1994). For our purposes, the Yankelovich MONITOR conclusions are the most relevant in these charts because they represent self-identified individuals based on the study's findings *as a national average.* (In reality, to be very specific, the largest cities tend to have a geographic average closer to 9 percent and the rural areas around 3 percent. See Figure 3.1 for the exact percentage that should be applied to each city population based on the rate of self-identification according to Yankelovich.)

In addition to a sampling of population estimates as cited in Table 3.3, I've also compiled a nuts-and-bolts review of all the studies I believe to bear the most relevance to gay and lesbian marketplace issues.

The Defense Department Research, 1992

The report's official name was: Sexual Orientation and U.S. Military Personnel Policy: Options and Assessment. National Defense Research Institute MR-323-OSD.[3]

This highly publicized study did not conduct any laboratory or field research on homosexuality of its own. It analyzed existing research, which it chose using a stringent set of criteria based on generalizable sampling methodology, and then drew conclusions based on an overall assessment of the chosen reports.

TABLE 3.3. Range of U.S. Gay and Lesbian Population Estimates by Race and Religion

1990 Census* Race (%)	Population*	10% Kinsey 1948	3.6% Harris 1988	1% Guttmacher 1993	6% Yankelovich 1994
White (80.3%)	199,686,070	19,968,607	7,188,699	1,996,861	11,981,164
Black (12.1%)	29,986,060	2,998,606	1,079,498	299,861	1,799,164
American Indian, Eskimo, or Aleut (0.8%)	1,959,234	195,923	70,532	19,592	117,554
Asian or Pacific Islander (2.9%)	7,273,662	727,366	261,852	72,737	436,420
Other (3.9%)	9,804,847	980,485	352,974	98,048	588,291
Total	248,709,873	24,870,987	8,953,555	2,487,099	14,922,593
Hispanic origin (9.0%)**	22,354,059	2,235,406	804,746	223,541	1,341,244

1990 Census* Religion (%)	Population*	10% Kinsey 1948	3.6% Harris 1988	1% Guttmacher 1993	6% Yankelovich 1994
Protestant (61%)	151,713,023	15,171,302	5,461,669	1,517,130	9,102,781
Roman Catholic (25%)	62,177,468	6,217,747	2,238,389	621,775	3,730,648
Jewish (2%)	4,974,197	497,420	179,071	49,742	298,452
Other (5%)	12,435,494	1,234,549	447,678	124,355	746,130
None (7%)	17,409,691	1,740,969	626,749	174,097	1,044,581
Total	248,709,873	24,870,987	8,953,555	2,487,099	14,922,592

*Source: Johnson, Otto, ed. (1994). *1994 Information Please Almanac.* Boston: Houghton Mifflin.
**Persons of Hispanic origin can be of any race.

FIGURE 3.1. Percentage of Self-Identification by Population Size

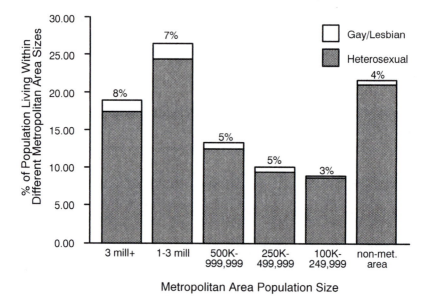

Metropolitan Area Population Size

Note: Displays the percentage of gays and lesbians in each metropolitan area according to size. For instance, 8 percent of the population in metropolitan areas of three million and greater population identify themselves as gay or lesbian.

The Rand report was sponsored by the Office of the Secretary of Defense under Rand's National Defense Research Institute, a federally funded research and development center supported by the Office of the Secretary of Defense (at the time Les Aspin) and the Joint Chiefs of Staff.

Five studies of sexuality were cited in the Rand Report, including sample characteristics, prevalence of same-gender sexual contact, methods of data collection, and response rates. The studies are:

- The National Opinion Research Council
- The General Social Survey Study
- Louis Harris and Associates
- Research Triangle Institute
- National Survey of Men

Table 3.4 illustrates the basic conclusions that these studies came to regarding "prevalence of same-gender sexual contact" which, as I've argued, is significantly different from individuals who self-identify as being gay or lesbian within a consumer research study.

The Kinsey Research, 1948

Wardell B. Pomeroy writes in his book, *Dr. Kinsey and the Institute for Sex Research*, "It is fair to say that Kinsey brought sex out of the bedroom and into the world's parlor. If he did not succeed in making it completely respectable, he laid the foundation for the greater freedom of sexual behavior and the far better understanding of it that we have today."[4]

A portion of Dr. Kinsey's conclusion on homosexuality was that about 10 percent of the males in his study reported to have had exclusively same-gender sex within a given period of three years. However, only 4 percent claimed to have been exclusively homosexual for the majority of their adult lives.

Dr. Kinsey also concluded that the incidence of homosexuality among females was roughly one-third to one-half that of men. He had intended to do more comprehensive studies on women but died in 1956 before the research was completed.

The common 10 percent figure heard in relationship to gay and lesbian population estimates is only applicable to men, at best, and is highly uncorrelatable to the national population forty years later for both sexes.

Still, Kinsey's qualitative and quantitative research on men has its strengths and so the conclusions he arrived at regarding population percentages overall should not be excluded when observing consumer markets in large urban areas. This is especially worth noting since Kinsey's methodology utilized face-to-face interviews, which usually reduces the number of people willing to identify as being exclusively homosexual. Yet Kinsey still came up with relatively high percentages of homosexual conduct for his time—which mirrors studies conducted in just the past few years. For this reason, I presented his analysis as a best-case scenario in Table 3.4.

Dr. Kinsey's report actually had many strengths despite the fact that his convenience sampling method did not meet the standards of

TABLE 3.4. Estimates of Homosexual Behavior from U.S. Probability Studies

Study	Sample Characteris- tics	Prevalence of Same-Gender Sexual Contact		Methods of Data Collection	Response Rate
		Male	Female		
National Opinion Research Council, (NORC) 1970 (Fay et al., 1989)	1,450 men ages 21 and older	Since age 20		SAQ following face-to-face interview	N/A
		6.7%	N/A		
		Last year			
		1.6-2.0%	N/A		
General Social Survey (GSS)* 1989-91	1,564 men 1,963 women ages 18 and older	Since age 18		SAQ following face-to-face interview	74%-78% (1988-1991)
		5.0%	3.5%		
	1,941 men 2,163 women ages 18 and older	Last year			
		2.2%	0.7%		
Louis Harris & Associates, 1988 (Taylor, 1993)	739 men 409 women ages 16 to 50	Last 5 years		SAQ following face-to-face interview; same-sex interviewer	67%
		4.4%	3.6%		
		Last year			
		3.5%	2.9%		
		Last month			
		1.8%	2.1%		
Research Triangle Institute (Rogers & Turner, 1991)	660 male residents of Dallas County, TX, ages 21-54	Last 10 years		SAQ	88%
		8.1%	N/A		
		Last year			
		4.6%	N/A		
National Survey of Men (NSM-1) (Billy et al., 1993)	3,321 men ages 20-39	Last 10 years		Face-to-face interview; female interviewers	70%
		2.3%	N/A		

Source: Rand Corporation (1992). *Sexual orientation and U.S. military personnel policy: Options and assessment.* National Defense Research Institute MR-343-0SD.

Notes: N/A = Not available
SAQ = Self-administered questionnaire

*Prevalence of male and female homosexuality calculated at Rand from General Social Surveys (Davis and Smith, 1991).

the Rand Corporation for the U.S. Department of Defense study. Among them, it had an extremely large sample size (12,000 participants) and extremely comprehensive questioning, covering an extraordinary minimum of 350 items and in some cases as many as 521. It is one of the most comprehensive studies of male sexuality ever conducted in history.[5]

The impeccable standards that Dr. Kinsey employed in his testing techniques are probably best captured in the words of Wardell B. Pomeroy, one of Dr. Kinsey's closest research associates:

> We asked our questions directly without hesitancy or apology. Kinsey correctly pointed out that if we were uncertain or embarrassed in our questioning we could not expect to get anything but a corresponding response. Unlike previous researchers, we did not say "touching yourself" when we meant masturbation, or "relations with other persons" when sexual intercourse was intended. "Evasive terms invite dishonest answers," was Kinsey's dictum. We also never asked whether a subject had ever engaged in a particular activity; we assumed that everyone had engaged in everything, and so we began by asking when he had first done it. Thus the subject who might want to deny an experience had a heavier burden placed on him, and since he knew from the way the question was asked that it would not surprise us if he had done it, there seemed little reason to deny it.
>
> . . . We looked our subjects squarely in the eye and fired the questions at them as fast as we could. These were two of our best guarantees against falsifying . . .[6]

Dr. Kinsey's work, of course, does not cover consumer-related behavior nor does it reflect recent contemporary sexual values in men. It has also been criticized by others (besides the Rand Corporation) for its use of convenience sampling rather than random sampling.

Unfortunately, his contributions to this day continue to be erroneously used by the press and activists to make arguments (mainly the out-of-context use of the 10 percent figure) that simply do not apply to women.

The Janus Research, 1992

The Janus Report was published in 1993 by researchers Samuel and Cynthia Janus.[7] Its research was derived from a substantially large sample size, 4,550 participants: 1,335 men and 1,384 women.

Each respondent was presented with anonymous questionnaires concerning "homosexual experiences" (research suggests an increased likelihood of disclosure when anonymity is allowed); and each participant was given the opportunity to "identify" as either homosexual or bisexual in addition to revealing specific sexual behavior.

The Janus report was not released early enough to be included in Rand's Sexual Orientation and U.S. Military Personnel Policy, but its conclusions are not likely to have changed Rand's final report in any significant way.

In the Janus study, participants were given a face-to-face personal interview prior to being handed an anonymous questionnaire with more controversial questions. Some researchers have suggested that this process may have created suspicion in participants' response to sensitive questions in the anonymous questionnaire.

In general, however, the Janus Report is among the most important and most significant of contemporary sexual research. When read in its entirety, the overall findings may provide significant insight to gay and lesbian consumer behavior.

The report concluded that 22 percent of males and 17 percent of females claimed having experienced at least one same-sex encounter in their lives. Of those responding, 9 percent of males identified as homosexual or bisexual and 5 percent of females as homosexual or bisexual.

The Guttmacher Institute, 1993

The Alan Guttmacher Institute conducted a study titled "The Sexual Behavior of Men in the United States,"[8] (analyzed by the Battelle Research Center), which was released in 1992. Although the study was not conducted specifically to determine the number of self-identified gay men in the United States or even the incidence of male-to-male sexual contact, it still received much play in the media because of its controversial conclusion that only 1 percent of its participants identified themselves as gay.

This conclusion was not surprising since most of the respondents were approached door-to-door in mainly suburban areas of the United States where gay and lesbian Americans are least likely to disclose their sexual identities.

Rivendell Marketing and The Simmons Research, 1997

Rivendell Marketing is a specialized firm of national advertising representatives with a track record in the domestic gay and lesbian marketplace. In association with a number of gay and lesbian newspapers, Rivendell contracts Simmons Market Research every few years to survey a very select group of gay and lesbian consumers who report that they regularly read publications represented nationally by Rivendell.

This particular research is important and useful as a starting point, but represents the consumer views and behaviors of only a modest proportion of the overall potential universe of gay consumers nationally. The gay and lesbian publications participating in the most recent Simmons study have formed a network called The National Gay Newspaper Guild (NGNG).[9]

The NGNG includes gay and lesbian publications across the United States including *The Southern Voice* (Atlanta), *Bay Area Reporter* (San Francisco), *Bay Windows* (Boston), *Dallas Voice, Frontiers* (LA), *The Houston Voice, Philadelphia Gay News, The New York Blade* (New York City), *The Washington Blade* (DC), *The Weekly News* (Florida), *The Windy City Times* (Chicago), the *Gay and Lesbian Times* (San Diego), and *The Weekly News* (Miami).

In addition to the NGNG network, Rivendell marketing also represents over 150 other important gay publications in the United States—many of which have conducted independent research of their readerships. Rivendell Marketing was launched over fifteen years ago by the late Joe DiSabato, a former music industry promotions specialist.

Gay and lesbian newspaper publishing grew enormously during the 1970s, and by the beginning of the 1980s, every major American city had a least one regularly published gay and lesbian news publication. Several had two. Rivendell Marketing was especially influential in helping keep a number of these gay and lesbian publications supplied with various kinds of advertising (some more than others).

As Rivendell Marketing grew and gained acceptance by the gay and lesbian news publishing industry, it also began attracting the attention of a number of high-caliber advertisers. Some launched large campaigns with Rivendell, including one for the movie *Making Love,* and also a campaign for Merck Sharp Dome in its promotion of the then-new hepatitis vaccine. There were even focus groups conducted for (what was then called) the Gay and Lesbian Press Association.

Rivendell Marketing has provided advertisers and publishers with a much-needed service in gay and lesbian advertising—allowing interested advertisers to reach the news-oriented, gay and lesbian publishing market quickly and efficiently. Likewise, they help local gay and lesbian news publications make themselves known as a group (in a more national way) in the "not easily distracted" New York media and advertising world.

For a while, Rivendell Marketing also handled a sizable portion of advertising for the gay and lesbian telephone provider service industry (phone sex). Rivendell still handles "a fair amount" of this business, but concedes that the industry's growth has probably "leveled off."

Rivendell Marketing's gross billings exceeded the $1 million mark for the first time in 1990 and surged past $2 million the following year—in part because the marketplace was enjoying an overall explosion, but also because the pharmaceutical company Burroughs Wellcome had begun its controversial HIV-related advertising campaign in association with other groups. Advertisements were displayed in many gay and lesbian publications and even in bus terminals in major cities across the United States.

Many read between the lines, though, and saw it as a campaign to essentially promote the use of the drug AZT. Burroughs Wellcome's campaign was one of the most expensive advertising buys in gay media history. Yet, the long-term efficacy of the drug's usefulness was one of the most hotly debated subjects among activists and individuals living with AIDS within the gay and lesbian community.

The Simmons data, although often used erroneously by media and activists to represent the national gay and lesbian population as a whole, actually is one of the best representations of America's more affluent gay and lesbian communities: readers of publications that are part of the National Gay Newspaper Guild and readers of publications that Rivendell represents.

The most current Simmons Market Research demographics of the National Gay Newspaper Guild Readers follows here:[10]

National Gay Newspaper Guild Survey

Gender
84.7 percent Male
15.3 percent Female

Age	Percentages
18-35	34.97
18-49	83.03
25-34	30.39
25-54	85.60
35-44	35.47
45-54	19.74

Education

- 65.04 percent have graduated a four-year college or more
- 19.3 percent have master's degrees
- 7.8 percent have doctoral degrees

Employment

- 86.8 percent are employed
- 53.61 percent professional/managerial
- 13.88 percent are employed in top management
- $47,090.00 average individual income
- 57.29 percent have individual incomes over $30,000
- 27.10 percent have individual incomes over $50,000
- 82.22 have household incomes over $30,000
- 58.18 percent have household incomes over $50,000

Readership Statistics

- Number of last six issues read/looked at: 5.13 (mean)
- Total amount of time spent with last issue: 46.46 minutes (mean)
- Total readers per copy: 2.26

- Combined NGNG circulations: 325,500
- Combined NGNG readerships: 735,630

Advertising Impact

- 93.69 percent are likely to use product/service advertised
- 90.12 percent are likely to purchase product/services of national businesses advertised

Miscellaneous

- 56.1 percent of respondents purchased condoms/contraceptives in the past twelve months.

Guild Readers versus General Population

- 2.9 times more likely to own a cassette deck
- 2.7 times more likely to own a CD player
- 5.9 times more likely to own a home theatre audio system
- 3.6 times more likely to own a minidisc player
- 5.6 times more likely to own a laptop computer
- 8 times more likely to own a notebook computer

Overlooked Opinions, 1989

Overlooked Opinions is a gay- and lesbian-oriented consumer research firm in Chicago, Illinois. There's not sufficient reason to believe that any marketer would not benefit from at least testing the results of an Overlooked Opinions survey—especially since their researchers claim their participants to be so affluent.

However, the company has taken some criticism from within the gay and lesbian business community regarding their research conclusions and their methodology—particularly over a $514 billion figure the firm has claimed as the size of the gay and lesbian economy nationwide.

In an interview with an Overlooked Opinions associate who has since left the company, the database panel of participants was said to be over 200,000 people (combined telephone and mail). Unfortunately, Overlooked Opinions does not sell or rent its list of sample participants, nor will they make available any of the names of their clients—which makes independent verification of their methodology somewhat problematic, and no doubt has fueled the controversy over their numbers.

The specific controversy concerns their figure of $514 billion, which was picked up and reported by the national press and electronic media until about 1993 without serious scrutiny and independent citing of other sources of opinion. When pressed on the legitimacy of the $514 billion number and how it was arrived at, an Overlooked Opinions representative who requested anonymity simply said they evaluated all the popular gay and lesbian research studies, including the 1990 Census data and a number of other factors—"but basically formulated Kinsey's basic estimate of what he believed the gay and lesbian population size to be (roughly 10 percent) in association with a trade secret" they weren't "interested in releasing."[11]

Technically speaking, it is conceivable that the gay and lesbian market is in fact worth tens of billions of dollars annually when considering all forms of financial activity. And since the African-American and Hispanic consumer markets are currently rated in hundreds of billions, there is not sufficient reason to believe that Overlooked Opinions' "trade secret" should necessarily be divulged just to alleviate what may be nothing more than competitive grumbling within the gay and lesbian business community.

The $514 billion number cannot actually be proven. Recent follow-up calls to Overlooked Opinions were not returned. However, one client of Overlooked Opinions who spoke only upon an agreement to anonymity expressed that Overlooked Opinions' work for his firm was "especially thorough, timely, and enlightening."

At a recent Overlooked Opinions presentation of their services to the New York Advertising and Communications Network (one of the largest gay and lesbian professional organizations in the United States) President Jeff Vitale was met with stern questioning from audience members after a rather dry presentation regarding the $514 billion figure. His response was ambiguous. After the presentation, one attendant remarked (about Vitale's answers), "I know obfuscation when I hear it." Another remarked that "he [Vitale] was just smart—he knows not to give away the store. . . ."

Still, many businesspeople in the gay and lesbian community are suspicious and especially annoyed when they hear religious and political fringe groups arguing that "gays and lesbians are affluent and not in need of special rights"—especially when such fringe groups have cited Overlooked Opinions' numbers as proof that gays and lesbians are not worthy of minority status.

Overlooked Opinions' official reaction to such allegations that they had unwittingly helped the radical right's cause was terse: "It's not our fault; it's poor planning on behalf of the gay and lesbian nonprofit groups that have let the radical right set the agenda. . . ."

In the final analysis, Overlooked Opinions has compiled an impressive list of gay and lesbian Americans. But most of their participants have been obtained through convenience sampling (at gay and lesbian business establishments, parades, etc.). As has been stated, convenience sampling does not give the most accurate picture of an entire population. Even Kinsey's historic sexual research was rejected by the Rand Corporation for the very same reasons: potentially biased sampling.

Still, Overlooked Opinions' database and services cannot be easily overlooked by marketers interested in investigating all their options.

The Voter News Service, 1992

On election day in 1992 the Voter News Service polled Americans with written questionnaires that were provided anonymously to people participating in the voting process at 300 different locations across the country. These locations were randomly selected.

In this study, 3.7 percent of the men and 2.8 percent of the women were determined to be self-identified gay or lesbian Americans, with 70 percent claiming to have voted for Clinton (less than 44 percent of all American voters actually cast a ballot for Clinton).

Although the sample was large, the results are not truly generalizable to the entire population because not everyone votes in an election. There was also concern that not everyone participating in the poll may have gotten to the end of the questionnaire where the question concerning gay/lesbian/bisexual appeared. However, only those who indicated on the form that they were gay were counted.

Overall, one of the most interesting findings stated in the final report was that "all voters believe by over 2 to 1 that government should promote traditional family values, while gays and lesbians believe by 2 to 1 that government should not promote one set of values over another."[12] In addition, the report stated that "There were no differences between gays and lesbians on the condition of the economy and they both had the same resistance to an increase in taxes, although gays and lesbians were more willing to accept increases for better health care. Gays and lesbians were also found to be more likely to pay attention to the candidates' wives and the conventions." Evidence was also cited that gays and lesbians were more active in the 1992 campaign and that they were three times as likely to wear a campaign button as were heterosexuals.

The National Health and Social Life Survey, 1992

The National Health and Social Life Survey was conducted in 1992 by the National Opinion Research Center at the University of Chicago.[13] It included a random sample of 3,432 U.S. residents and found 2.8 percent of the men and 1.4 percent of the women self-identifying as gay.

Interestingly, this study found what other studies such as the Yankelovich and Simmons Market Research Survey found: that gay men and lesbians are more likely to self-identify in the cities. In fact, this particular survey found that 10.2 percent more men and 2.1 percent more women were likely to self-identify in the twelve largest metropolitan areas of country than in the suburbs.

Newsweek Poll, 1994

This poll was conducted for *Newsweek* magazine. The principal research was handled by Princeton Research Associates and cited over 1,400 lesbians and gay men for a feature article titled "Homophobia, Politics, and Issues."[14] Participants for this study were obtained through a random sampling search of a gay and lesbian population database owned and managed by Strubco, New York City.

The study found that over 70 percent of Americans self-identifying as gay or lesbian also claimed to be Democrats, with nearly 80 percent indicating that they voted for Clinton.

Unfortunately, the sample was probably biased because it was largely composed of individuals who have given to gay and lesbian charities or who have purchased products from gay and lesbian identified or owned companies, thereby potentially skewing the sample in a more affluent direction, as Overlooked Opinions panel participants are also more likely to test out upscale.

The National Gay and Lesbian Task Force, 1996

Readers should note that this study was based on the same exit polling that was conducted during the 1992 election by the Voter News Service as described above, and even though it is not generalizable to the national population, it still is an important, statistically significant study giving insights to marketers. It is telling that most news organizations purchased the poll in 1992 but basically only reported the one fact that 70 percent of gays and lesbians voted for Clinton.

However, once the data was more closely analyzed it was then presented to the public at large through the task force's efforts and the help they received from pollster Murray Edelman, who conducted the poll for Voter Research and Surveys. Perhaps most important, it was made clear that gay voters are younger than nongay ones.

According to the task force data, sixty-one percent of gay voters were under 40, compared with 44 percent of nongays; 30 percent were under 30, compared with 20 percent. And among older voters, only 11 percent of gays were 60 and over, compared with 21 percent of nongays. The figures suggest that younger people are more likely to indicate that they are gay. A complete copy of this study is available from the Policy Institute of the National Gay and Lesbian Task Force, Washington, DC.

The Human Rights Campaign/Lake Research Study, 1996

This survey's findings were based on questions added to a series of polls conducted by the ICR Survey Research Group for Lake Research and the Human Rights Campaign.[15] ICR contacted 365 self-identifying gays, lesbians, or bisexuals by telephone from May to September 1996. The maximum margin of error was 5.2 percentage points.

Employment and Income

According to those sampled, gays and lesbians earn wages similar to those of most Americans. Forty percent earn $25,000 or less, 35 percent earn between $25,000 and $50,000, and a fifth earn over $50,000. More than six in ten are employed full time. While a majority (61%) have shared their orientation with co-workers, a majority (53%) have not shared their orientation with their employers.

Household Information

Of those contacted, most consider themselves single, but a majority now live or have lived with a partner in a serious relationship. Almost half of self-identified gays and lesbians are currently involved in a long-term monogamous relationship. Twenty-two percent have children living in their households.

Region

About a third indicated that they live in the South, a quarter in the West and Northeast, and about a fifth live in the Midwest.

Ideology

The survey found that a majority of those sampled consider themselves liberal. Nearly a majority are Democrats, with a third independent. The poll also found that gay men and lesbians are similar to other Americans with regard to the issues they care about. A total of 24 percent cited crime and drugs as the issues they worry about the most; 17 percent cited jobs and the economy; 16 percent said health care; and 15 percent listed education as their number one concern. A complete analysis of the research, including graphs and charts, is available at the HRC Web site at http://www.hrc.org.

The Greenfield Online/Spare Parts Study, 1998

This groundbreaking study was conducted by Greenfield Online, Inc., the pioneer of marketing research using the Internet, in partnership with Spare Parts, Inc., a consulting company specializing in lesbian- and gay-focused consumer marketing. Having created an ongoing panel just for gay and lesbian research, Greenfield and Spare Parts hope to demystify a largely underserved area with a panel planned to be over 5,000 in size by the end of 1999. The first study of 948 respondents provided detailed information about their buying habits, travel plans, what publications they read, and hundreds of other facts about their daily lives.

As with all studies, interpretation depends on how you look at the numbers and whether you make logical comparisons between sample groups and other studies. For perspective, the general findings of the Greenfield/Spare Parts study (July 1998) are provided along with the annual benchmark Georgia Tech Internet study of the general population for the same period (GVU Ninth Survey April 1998, Table 3.5).

The findings tend to parallel in some ways what was learned in the groundbreaking 1994 Yankelovich MONITOR's Gay Lesbian Perspective (see Chapter 4)—that gay and lesbian consumers as a group do not necessarily earn more than their heterosexual counterparts, nor do they always lead more affluent lives.

In the case of the Greenfield study, according to the conclusions reached by the researchers, the Internet proved to be an effective way to reach what has traditionally been a hard-to-find segment of society. "Many lesbians and gays prefer not to identify themselves as such for a variety of reasons, but this study has shown dramatically that our community is out of the cybercloset in large numbers. We now have a powerful way to create an ongoing conversation," says Scott Seitz, a managing partner of Spare Parts. "This will be an important ongoing discussion because we plan to field our study four times a year—an easy goal for Internet-based research."

This is a particularly important benchmark study for the lesbian and gay Internet community—one that allows marketers more ready access to a broader pool of gay people while using methodologies acceptable to research professionals as well as the lesbian and gay community.

Lesbians and gays who regularly use the Internet and participated in this online survey responded to a battery of attitudinal questions. These responses were subjected to factor analysis and six distinct clusters emerged, which are characterized by Greenfield Online as follows:

> Life Enthusiasts
> The Suits
> Settled at Home
> Silent Conformers
> Self-Stylists
> The Vanguards

By examining the beliefs, attitudes, and lifestyles of the different groups in conjunction with their demographics and likely purchasing behavior, one can learn about and focus on specific segments of the lesbian and gay population.

According to the study, lesbian and gay consumers with Internet access say they spend an average of three hours a day on-line, excluding e-mail. Some 80 percent own personal computers and 19 percent indicated they plan to buy one in the next six months.

Characteristics similar to the general market:

- Surprisingly, gays and lesbians who regularly use the Internet are as settled as other Internet users, with 55 percent of men and 68 percent of lesbians describing themselves as monogamous.
- Thirteen percent already have children, while 17 percent are planning to adopt.
- Brand conscious and thrifty, 49 percent of lesbians and gays describe themselves as "budget conscious when shopping."
- Average household income is only slightly higher at $57,300 versus $52,000 for the general Internet population (GVU).
- Gays and lesbians are as likely as the general population to have had at least some college, but are over twice as likely to have completed a doctoral or law degree.

Key areas of difference:

- Lesbian/gay alliance is strong in this community. Ninety-two percent agree they represent "a powerful economic force" and 80 percent say they prefer to buy from companies who advertise in the gay market.

- Gay media is very relevant and both national and local publications are consumed at a rate higher than *any* traditional media for community news and information.
- Local publications are not always accessible, and 29 to 40 percent of lesbians and gays in this sample depend on the Internet for community news and information.
- Ninety percent say it is important for them to work in a safe, gay-friendly environment.
- ABC, the network that hosted *Ellen*, is the most-watched network in the gay community.

Methodology for the study:

- The sample of 948 respondents was drawn from the specialist lesbian and gay on-line panel members, who have been recruited by Greenfield Online to participate in on-line surveys.
- Respondents were invited by e-mail to go to a password-protected area of the Greenfield Online Web site to complete the survey on-line. The fieldwork was conducted between June 26 and July 14, 1998.
- The questionnaire for the survey was drafted by Greenfield Online, Inc. in consultation with Spare Parts, Inc.
- The study covered:

  —Demographics
  —Lifestyles, activities, values, and attitudes
  —Media and entertainment habits
  —Internet and telecom usage
  —Technology ownership
  —Intended purchases, including a variety of durable and consumer goods

THE OVERALL PICTURE

Although other important studies do exist on gay and lesbian sexuality, it is my opinion that they contribute little toward understanding gay and lesbian Americans qualitatively as consumers. For instance, the National Opinion Research Center in Chicago conducted a number of important surveys between 1988 and 1992 that included many questions about homosexuality, yet many people

TABLE 3.5. Findings of the Greenfield Online/Spare Parts Study and Georgia Tech Study

	Lesbian/Gay Internet Population Sample Lesbian & Gay Market Study, July 1998 (n = 948)		General Internet Population Sample GVU Ninth Survey, April 1998 (n = 10,109)	
Gender	Male	68%	Male	59%
	Female	32%	Female	41%
		100%		100%
Age	Under 18	1%	Under 16	2%
	18-24	18%	16-25	24%
	25-34	38%	26-35	26%
	35-44	28%	36-45	21%
	45-54	13%	46-55	17%
	55-64	3%	56-65	6%
	65-74	1%	66 or older	2%
			No response	2%
		100%		100%
Average	34.2		35.1	
Education	High school or less	11%	Grammar/high school	13%
	Some college (1-3 years)	46%	Vocational/technical/some college	37%
	Graduated 4-year college	20%	College	30%
	Some postgraduate	8%		
	Master's degree	10%	Master's degree	14%
	Doctorate or law degree	5%	Doctoral	2%
	Refused/not stated	0%	Professional/special/other	4%
		100%		100%
Status	Married	3%	Married	44%
	Living in domestic partnership	39%	Living with another	8%
	Single	51%	Single	36%
	Separated/divorced/widowed	7%	Separated/divorced/widowed	11%
	Refused/not stated	0%	Refused/not stated	2%
		100%		100%
Annual household income before taxes	Under $25,000	17%	Under $10,000	4%
	$25,000-44,999	29%	$10,000-$19,999	6%
	$45,000-64,999	22%	$20,000-$29,999	9%
	$65,000-84,999	13%	$30,000-$39,999	12%
	$85,000-99,999	7%	$40,000-$49,999	11%
	$100,000-149,999	7%	$50,000-$74,999	21%
	$150,000+	4%	$75,000-$99,999	10%
			Over $100,000	11%
	Refused/not stated	1%	Not specified	17%
		100%		100%
Average	$57,300		$52,000	

TABLE 3.5 (continued)

	Lesbian/Gay Internet Population Sample Lesbian & Gay Market Study, July 1998 (n = 948)			General Internet Population Sample GVU Ninth Survey, April 1998 (n = 10,109)	
Ethnicity	Caucasian	85%	Caucasian/White		88%
	African American	3%	African American		2%
	Hispanic/Latin American	3%	Hispanic/Latino		2%
	Native American	2%	Indigenous or Aboriginal		1%
	Oriental Asian	1%	Asian/Pacific Islander		2%
	Middle Eastern Asian	0%			
	Afro-Hispanic	0%			
	Afro-Asian	0%			
	Other	4%	Other		2%
	Refused/not stated	1%	Not stated		2%
		100%			100%
Region	Pacific	22%	Pacific		22%
	Mountain	6%	Mountain		6%
	West North Central	7%	West North Central		6%
	West South Central	10%	West South Central		9%
	East North Central	14%	East North Central		13%
	East South Central	5%	East South Central		5%
	South Atlantic	17%	South Atlantic		22%
	Middle Atlantic	13%	Middle Atlantic		13%
	New England	7%	New England		6%
		100%			100%
Sexual orientation	Heterosexual		Heterosexual		87%
	Gay male	0%	Gay male		3%
	Lesbian	64%	Lesbian		1%
	Bisexual	27%	Bisexual		3%
	Transgender	9%	Transgender		0%
	Not stated	0%	Not stated		5%
		0%			
		100%			100%

refused to respond to any of the questions about sexuality. Other studies conducted by universities and political think tanks have also contributed greatly to our understanding of sexuality, but none of them deviate substantially or call into question the quantitative debates over gay and lesbian population size any more than those indicated above.

To date, by far the most conclusive and verifiable national gay and lesbian population figure, based on random sampling conducted in the home by a widely respected commercial research firm in the United States and weighted against the 1990 census data is the 1994-issued Yankelovich MONITOR Gay and Lesbian Perspective.

In that study it was clearly demonstrated by Yankelovich researchers that Americans are willing to self-identify as gay or lesbian, if asked, at levels as high as 9 percent in large cities, and 2 to 4 percent in rural and suburban areas. This gives us a total national gay and lesbian population average of about 6 percent in the United States.

Setting the numbers debate aside, it is really the highly sophisticated qualitative information contained in the Yankelovich MONITOR Gay and Lesbian Perspective that marketers should be enthused about because it tells us new information about gay and lesbian purchasing behavior and what motivates their product decision making processes.

The study also reveals compelling developments taking place within the national gay and lesbian community—a community totaling a minimum of 15 million self-identified American consumers who are actually looking for new products and services produced by modern, more contemporary-thinking companies willing to support them in their quest to uphold equality for all Americans—gay or straight.

The Yankelovich MONITOR's
Gay and Lesbian Perspective, 1994

In the summer of 1993, I proposed that a number of institutions (including universities and advertising agencies) consider conducting an intensive, groundbreaking study on the rapid emergence of gay and lesbian consumerism in America. It would have to be independently based on nationally conducted focus groups, or a battery of randomly selected respondents that could be scientifically generalized to the national population. It would investigate and analyze, for the first time, the extraordinary nature of gay and lesbian consumer and cultural attitudes in America, rather than the mere incidence of a particular kind of sexual behavior.

The methodology and handling of the research had to be high-profile enough that anyone familiar with marketing science would see its immediate value and widespread application in business—particularly in tracking consumer perceptions. It had to have a usefulness to AT&T and General Motors; but it also needed to intrigue activists as well as generate interest in academic circles.

Yankelovich Partners, Inc. turned out to be that company.

In June of 1994, the first Yankelovich MONITOR's Perspective on Gays/Lesbians was completed and made commercially available. No other report or study of gay and lesbian Americans, as consumers, has ever been conducted similar to the one accomplished by Yankelovich.

The final report, which is officially called the Yankelovich MONITOR Perspective on Gays/Lesbians, may not be an infallible document. However, for gay and lesbian Americans it is an historical accomplishment. And for American business, and particularly for marketers, it is a much-awaited and long-needed high-tech instrument now confirming that the adult gay and lesbian population in the United States is a distinct, highly influential, and well-identified consumer group.

The Yankelovich investigation into gay and lesbian consumer motivations sets a significant market precedent; but it also demonstrates why more research needs to be conducted. Its shortcomings notwithstanding, the study has in many ways helped to unmask the social myths about gay and lesbian people—allowing more people in business to better discern what gay and lesbian consumers want from the companies they do business with. Today, it is specifically the increasing visibility of gays and lesbians—both in the media and the workplace—in combination with a growing portfolio of new research about them, that is allowing the remaining myths of the twentieth century to simply evaporate. In fact, it was this increased visibility in the marketplace that helped bring about Yankelovich Partners' acknowledgement that such a study should be conducted.

Now, rather than dredging through the remaining vestiges of gay and lesbian stereotypes, business and government are better served by an investigation into how the effects of such myths have commercially segregated gays and lesbians as individual consumers and influenced the way in which they are now participating in the overall economy. To help understand some major distinctions between self-identified gay and lesbian consumers and heterosexual consumers, a brief summary of the social climate currently prevalent among the total population of American consumers is provided in Chapter 4.

This information—which has been tracked since 1971—is part of an ongoing study by Yankelovich Partners, simply known as the Yankelovich MONITOR, which businesses, both in the United States and all over the world, turn to regularly for its sophisticated analysis and unique perspective of American consumer behavior.

The underlying methodological assumption of the MONITOR is that traditional economic and demographic predictors such as those tracked by the government are insufficient for a complete under-standing of marketplace behavior. Therefore, in addition to measuring traditional demographics, the Yankelovich MONITOR is designed to quantitatively measure social attitudes, values, perceptions, and behaviors, thus sketching a more complete portrait of the consumer.

The Yankelovich MONITOR research cited in this book (and the Yankelovich MONITOR Perspective on Gays/Lesbians as originally conducted for this book), was collected by means of a ninety-minute personal interview conducted in the homes of a nationally represen-tative sample of 2500 consumers over the age of sixteen. Interviewing was conducted door-to-door in 315 locations across the continental United States and is balanced (weighted) to mirror U.S. census demo-graphic characteristics. Total error due to sampling is plus or minus 4 percent.

In an effort to provide a broad picture of what is going on in the minds of American consumers, the Yankelovich MONITOR covers a wide variety of subjects, many of them extremely sensitive. In order to ensure accurate information on these issues, a number of techniques are constructed to alleviate embarrassment or anxiety on the part of Yankelovich's respondents.

Two are particularly worth noting:

- The one-and-one-half-hour questionnaire is administered in the respondent's home—a secure environment controlled by the respondent.
- Sensitive topics, such as those dealing with individual identity, are placed in a spiral binder of exhibit cards. For such ques-tions, each respondent is instructed to turn to the appropriate card and asked to indicate only the number that corresponds to the responses they choose. In this way, respondents disclose information confidentially.

Regarding statistical significance and the gay/lesbian sample of the Yankelovich data cited here, approximately 6 percent of the 2,503 respondents sixteen years of age and older is represented (n = 148). The sample was identified by means of an item in the 1993 Yankelo-vich MONITOR's interview that asked respondents to choose from a list of fifty-two adjectives/phrases, items which the respondents believed best described them. The exact wording of the item used to identify respondents for this analysis was "gay/homosexual/lesbian." Researchers at Yankelovich Partners indicate that, for marketers, this self-identification technique may be more reliable than others that have been used to analyze the gay/lesbian population.

Magazine subscription lists or voluntary return mail questionnaires are neither random nor representative of the gay and lesbian population as a whole; they contain substantial bias and are not weighted to mirror U.S. census demographic characteristics. The value of the Yankelovich data and methodology is that it has identified only those consumers who are willing to acknowledge that they are gay or lesbian, and it has scientifically identified them using a random sampling formula that is generalizable to the entire population.

Further, Yankelovich respondents were not asked to divulge information about their sexual identity through a written questionnaire. Nor were they required to "check off any boxes" or write anything down on paper, or even answer any verbal questions about sexual behavior per se, during the interview process. They were simply given the opportunity to identify themselves as gay/lesbian/ homosexual by giving a number associated with one of the fifty-two listed descriptors that were presented to the respondent as a group in the form of a simple spiral binder of charts. As respondents flipped through the charts, they called out the corresponding code numbers next to those words that they believed described them.[16]

This sliver of difference in the Yankelovich methodology in questioning and identifying gay and lesbian participants regarding sexual identification may well be the driving determinant that resulted in an overall higher percentage of gays and lesbians being indicated over other studies to date. In any event, the Yankelovich study did not seek to determine sexual behavior; only self-disclosed sexual identity. Once the self-identified gay/lesbian/homosexual individuals were determined, we then looked at what characteristics, attitudes, beliefs, and values separated them from the overall sample—presumed to be largely heterosexual.

The conclusions are examined in the next chapter—the majority of which are both enlightening and useful.

Chapter 4

Understanding Pride and Pragmatism: A Marketer's View of Modern Gay and Lesbian Culture

The social values of human activities must be measured by many scales other than those which are available to the scientist.

Alfred Kinsey[1]

Study after study shows that Americans are fed up with the complicated. We want simplicity.[2]

In our desire to create more understanding, clarity, and comfort in our lives, a number of social and economic changes are making themselves painfully apparent, one of which is the wholesale disruption of the long sacrosanct institution of marriage.

In the past twenty-five years, heterosexual marriage has undergone enormous changes around the world. In the United States alone, the number of people getting married and staying married is confirmedly on the decline. The estimates vary, but the overall accepted divorce rate is now at about 50 percent. Getting out of a legal marriage is now literally as common as trying to stay in one.

In 1975, roughly 500,000 heterosexuals claimed to be living together, but unmarried. Today that number is a whopping six times larger, totaling over 3 million—as many as were merely "going steady" during the middle of the twentieth century.[3] In addition, it is now no longer safe to say that living together, out of wedlock, is a fad. Fads only last a few seasons. Nor would it be altogether fair to refer to such developments as "trends." Trends last several seasons. And, clearly, the decline of long-term legal marriages in the United States is something more than a mere trend.

America is experiencing an evolution in the status of heterosexual marriage—one of its most fundamental organizing principles of society. In fact, this evolution is occurring worldwide—in both industrialized and developing countries. As *The New York Times* recently noted, "Around the world, in rich and poor countries alike, the structure of family life is undergoing profound changes. . . . The reality is that trends like unwed motherhood, rising divorce rates, smaller households, and the feminization of poverty are not unique to America, but are occurring worldwide."[4]

One of the central forces behind these changes relates to the need for women to enter the workforce in order to continue providing a stable environment for children. In addition, cuts by governments in aid to dependent families is an increasing trend around the globe as are cuts to education in an attempt to repay national debts.

A report issued by the Population Council titled "Families in Focus" found that the stability of child support payments by fathers separated from children is also difficult to maintain in countries other than the United States. According to the *Times,* the report claimed "that among divorced fathers, three-quarters in Japan, almost two-thirds in Argentina, half in Malaysia and two-fifths in the United States do not pay child support."[5] As the report argued, there needs to be a rethinking of the "policies and programs to strengthen the father-child link . . . "

With all these changes occurring at an accelerated pace in the United States, clearly an entirely new array of consequences are being placed at our national doorstep. Still there are interesting parallels between the disruptions and stresses of marriage in America, and the isolation and stresses experienced by gay and lesbian people living in a predominantly heterosexual society.

Americans are all facing major changes related to economics; some we understand, many we are still seeking answers to. And obviously where one is financially situated determines how one relates to the social order. This, of course, does not always make for pleasant encounters amongst the citizenry.

ECONOMICS AND THE SEXUAL IDENTITY CRISIS

Consumers are constantly responding and reacting to a number of social stimuli—including, perhaps, most devisively, the pervasive idea that the attainment of wealth is necessarily a "good thing." Perhaps it is, or could one day be made to be. But surely the waning of hetero-sexual commitment to marriage and all that it entails is strongly related to the demands that the modern economic state continues to place on the individual's ability to feel worthy and secure.

The twentieth century has inflicted upon the American psyche nearly all possible stresses imaginable. We are now subconsciously trying to find ways to alleviate the pressure to get rich by seeking out new forms of expression—new ways of strengthening and re-inventing human identity, democratic idealism, and the "pursuit of happiness."

This search for more applicable values is particularly noticeable in the rhetoric of young gay and lesbian activists, who in their calls for same-sex marriage legislation are actually demanding what hetero-sexuals are ostensibly now having trouble maintaining. The ironies are everywhere: Single mothers getting kicked off welfare, gay and lesbian couples paying income taxes on domestic partner health benefit packages.

In the meantime, in the bigger social picture, we are all wrestling with an unpredictable world economy that seems destined to allow everything from dishpans, telephones, hair styling perm rods, and electrical extension cord prices to be determined in some neototal-itarian sweatshop deep in the heart of China.

Today, with everyone working, our product-laden households have been left literally abandoned in daytime suburbia.

Our cumulative waking hours are also now spent living and working differently—interacting, looking at, and responding to more aggressive and overly sexualized commercial imagery. And the images we see in advertising, television and films affect us greatly. They result in increased levels of stress and guilt about our individual relationships to the world's problems.

And as many middle-income earners work harder than the gener-ation before, plenty still awaken to find their money less valuable and the continued earning of it more problematic. We have social stresses, demands, health concerns, costs, and procedures that our parents didn't have to deal with. Our children know more about drugs, sex, and guns than we do. We're told that we can't trust our senses, that we can no longer eat what tastes good to us. We're even required by law to sort our trash differently.

The feeling we are left with is something I call "hypercomplexity"—a subtle and insidious kind of group fear. A fear that is hard to identify, hard to track. But we feel it in the shopping center parking lot where there are no trees. We feel it on Sunday afternoon after watching the morning news shows. We feel it when traffic doesn't move. We feel it when the phone answering machine isn't blinking with a message when we get home. We feel it when it is blinking. We feel it when we're uncertain about a product we're buying. We feel it even more when we try to understand the label.

National leaders urging us to return to patriarchal-based consumer economic units and family values rhetoric don't deal with hypercomplexity; they make it worse. And nobody is more aware of all this folly than gay and lesbian consumers themselves.

ADAPTATION AND CHANGE

Gay and lesbian Americans are masters at dealing with hypercomplexity. This is because they grew up learning to deal with fear every single day of their lives.

As children many are taunted and abused throughout their childhood. They have trouble finding common ground with their parents and church leaders. Gay and lesbian role models are nonexistent. Puberty is a nightmare. High school is a mental concentration camp.

Coping systems become keenly fine-tuned, warlike, cunning, and at times powerful. Self-defense, individual freedom, and high moral ground become your reason for living.

As the historian James M. Saslow, who wrote *Ganymede in the Renaissance: Homosexuality in Art and Society,* expressed in an interview with veteran *Advocate* journalist Mark Thompson, "I was a bookworm, not the least bit interested in sports, and very creative. . . . The word everybody always used to describe me was artistic. But there would be this slight pause before they said it, so I knew they weren't just talking about my ability to draw. There was something larger the word seemed to refer to, but people would never quite say it out loud."[6]

Traditionally, gay and lesbian individuals throughout history have been denied the right to participate in the majority of state- and church-sanctioned institutions and rituals—because such social monuments were designed to ensure the viability, livelihood, and longevity of heterosexually organized economic systems.

No doubt, much has changed. But in the United States, gay and lesbian Americans are still not federally protected from discrimination in employment, housing, insurance, or medical care. In fact, gay and lesbian Americans simply do not enjoy the same number of protections under the law as do heterosexuals. The reason for this is simple: gay and lesbian Americans are not heterosexual, not part of what was once a reigning decree of social order, the paradigm around which our economy has been organized for so long.

When gay and lesbian Americans travel abroad, they're often shocked to learn the degree to which gay and lesbian people from other countries enjoy more civil rights and legal protections than they do as Americans. This is particularly so in Denmark, Sweden, Holland, and Canada; and now, with the inclusion of the words "sexual orientation" in their new constitution, South Africa.

Moreover, gays and lesbians are very aware of the degree to which heterosexual Americans have misunderstood the gay and lesbian communities' perspective on equal rights legislation. Many straights aren't aware of the rage that exists toward gay and lesbian Americans, that they are routinely accused by political extremists of asking for special rights and perpetuating a "homosexual agenda." Gay people are scapegoated for our country's alleged decline of moral values and crumbling of family structures—yet gays and lesbians were never accepted as part of such structures to begin with!

For sure, gay and lesbian Americans laugh at such folly. And for historically documentable reasons: Many know full well that talk of the breakup of the family has been going on in the American press dating back as far as 1831 with the "new moral reform movements." During those times, there were even "societies" and "task forces" set up with the help of government to "stop prostitution" and "uphold" traditional values, yet underground economies forged around alcoholism and prostitution were quietly encouraged to flourish—just as drugs and alcoholism are allowed to flourish today.

Even the tired twentieth-century lament "Just say no" originated in the early days of the nineteenth century—yet few Americans realize it is just another coded statement revived 150 years later under Reaganomics.[7] "Just say no" was a failure then, just as it was a hundred years later during the Prohibition era, and as it is again, at the end of this century.

As heterosexual society has focused on staying consistent throughout the years, gay and lesbian social enclaves organized and began more conspicuously influencing arts and science, social politics, and now, consumer economics.

More Adaptation and More Change

Today, new ideas about the well-being of the individual are germinating out of the experiences of gay and lesbian consumers. As a traditionally invisible people, gay and lesbian Americans have had to custom-fashion and redirect their personal values and group understandings of the world around them toward a more common sense-oriented approach to modern life *as it really is for them*—out of sheer emotional and financial self-preservation. As John D'Emilio wrote in *Sexual Politics, Sexual Communities: The Making of a Homosexual Minority in the United States, 1940-1970:*

> In addition to the opprobrium emanating from religion, law, and medicine, American society at large revealed its disapproval of homosexual eroticism by sharply curtailing public discussion of the topic. . . .
> [Eventually] gay liberation affected the self-image even of those men and women who never joined a gay organization or participated in a demonstration. Its ideas permeated the subculture of lesbians and homosexuals so that pride and openness became common characteristically. . . . During the 1970s in virtually every area of American life, debates raged and battles were fought over homosexuality.[8]

With the passage of time, Harlem, Stonewall, the Women's Music Movement, the AIDS crisis, ACT UP (AIDS Coalition to Unleash Power), and the noise level of *Outweek* magazine (and—most importantly—the explosive growth of gay and lesbian-centered media it fueled over the past five years), the gay and lesbian community has begun spawning a new way of looking at its visual imagery, consumer economics, fiscal responsibility, public and private social relationships, and the passing down of values via a new set of community-based economic checks and balances.

The domestic partnership health insurance movement in America's largest corporations is just the beginning of this important new social movement (and it might be worth noting here that more unmarried heterosexual Americans take advantage of domestic partnership benefits than do gay and lesbian Americans).

In a sense, gay and lesbian consumers are more poised to place a greater emphasis on the sanctity, security, and opportunity of individuals in relation to sexual issues because they never bought into the fading myth that growing economies and strong patriarchal family units will lead us out of our social and environmental troubles. As Vice President Al Gore poignantly noted in *Earth in the Balance:*

> . . . Ultimately, part of the solution . . . may well lie in our ability to achieve a better balance between the sexes, leaving the dominant male perspective with a healthier respect for female ways of experiencing the world.
>
> . . . our hope as a civilization may well lie in our potential for adjusting to a health[ier] sense of ourselves as a truly global civilization, one with a mature sense of responsibility for creating new and generative relationships between ourselves and the earth.[9]

To be sure, in gay and lesbian America, family is not dead. It is powerfully alive, vibrant, moral, and generative. It is focused on individuality, diversity, affirmative opportunity, and a deep moral sense of balance between the spiritual, the environmental, and the economic.

This is not the "me generation" revisited. It is a wholesale rediscovery of one of our most original American values—that of individualism—a total shifting of the focus of responsibility away from outdated family structures back to individual structures—as envisioned during the early days of our republic: Freedom of the individual. Freedom of enterprise. Civic responsibility. Equal protection under the law.

That's ultimately what the gay and lesbian consumer revolution in America is all about. To obtain the exact same equal protection under the law for all gay and lesbian Americans that are currently enjoyed by all heterosexual Americans: a literal reawakening and call for a return to the most basic of all American values: freedom of the individual. And this is a revolution that may already be working with business—perhaps your competition—for change, change that is good for everyone. Because the new age of consumer individuality is all about inclusivity, affirmative opportunity, and civic responsibility. It is also pragmatic, morally driven, willing to boycott—and unstoppable.

The power of the mind-set of the gay or lesbian consumer and how he or she differs from the heterosexual consumer cannot be underestimated. It affects everything from their behavior at the cash register and their interaction with salespeople to the bank machines they use depending on the time of day. Companies marketing products and services to gays and lesbians need to be mindful of these differences.

CONTEXT MATTERS

Before examining some of the best statistical numbers compiled to date on gay and lesbian consumers, it is important to understand the data within the context of preidentified trends among the majority of American consumers' findings and analysis in a social climate overview.

In the Yankelovich overview, the following attitudinal and demographic trends among all Americans were cited as being of primary importance in the current social context of American life.[10]

Looking at America's Three-Generational Views of Life

Key areas of focus and concern among Americans are interpreted differently based on age and the associated historical experiences related to age. This has resulted in the evolutionary development of three distinct consumer population cohorts in the United States: the Mature Generation; Baby Boomers; and the so-called Generation X. Each of these groups contributes to the fragmenting process within the American consumer marketplace spectrum. Each group's worldview varies according to its own social and economic acculturational process within history.

Regarding their marketplace perspective, each of the three cohorts differ greatly—not only in their worldview, but their marketplace behavior as well. The groups are best characterized in the following way:

- The Mature Generation (ages fifty years and older) grew up with a range of memories: stories of the Depression, the effects of two World Wars, and McCarthyism, much of which taught them caution, thrift, playing by the rules, and living for tomorrow. Matures buy the "right thing," what someone "like me" is expected to have. Gender distinctions remain clear for them; women are responsible for shopping and all food and beverage decisions. Structure and order is important to them; change is perceived as threatening.

- The Baby Boomer Generation (ages thirty to forty-nine) came of age in an era of unparalleled prosperity and possibilities, from which they developed a psychology of entitlement and a "can-do" attitude that does not recognize limits. Boomers continue to focus on selective "what's right for me." They believe, with reason, that products are made and marketed to meet their own personal needs. Their current life stage makes them among the most stressed consumers (jobs and kids and personal lives). Leisure and relaxation are therefore particularly important to them.

- Generation X (ages sixteen to twenty-nine) has faced a difficult economy and a fiercely competitive environment throughout their lives. They have grown up to have a practical, cynical, and self-protective nature. Generation Xers worry about being able to get what they want and need, but they are ready to do what they must to succeed in the marketplace, as well as in other aspects of life. They feel that they "get no respect" from the marketplace, which focuses on the needs of the two previous generations. Xers are extremely worried about their personal futures, especially their ability to find and maintain jobs. Many have adopted a "live for today" attitude, especially with regard to leisure and fun, since the opportunities of today may not be available tomorrow.

Race and Ethnicity in America: A Melting Pot No Longer

Along with the three generational views of American consumers come cultural and economic dynamics that affect the fragmentation of the marketplace as well. These dynamics are informed, in part, by issues relating to race and ethnicity. For instance, African Americans will remain a constant 12 percent of the population; however, the Asian and Hispanic segments of the U.S. population will grow rapidly, both by birth and immigration. Considered together, this will mean one out of three Americans will belong to a "minority" group ten years after the turn of the century.

This development signals changes for everything from music and entertainment to food, cooking, and other characteristics of modern life that affect mainstream American culture (for instance, salsa now outsells ketchup in the United States).

In addition, today's immigrant populations, unlike earlier waves, have a different approach to assimilation:

- They wish to become American and to enjoy all the rights and responsibilities that this entails.
- They also desire to retain key elements of their national culture—most important, their native languages.

Bearing all these varying issues in mind—that gay and lesbian Americans also fit into Mature, Baby Boomer, and Generation X cohorts, and that they also contribute and respond to issues relating to the overall social climate, race, ethnicity, age, and experience—we are now ready to examine the emerging gay and lesbian attitudinal mind-set in modern America.

A GENERAL GAY AND LESBIAN
AMERICAN PROFILE

With the research conducted by Yankelovich Partners, it is now possible to better understand gay and lesbian consumers on a number of scientific, social, and economic frontiers. The first important phase of this research, completed in the summer of 1994, was conducted in collaboration for this book and based on the scientific analysis of a variety of social values among research respondents who identified themselves as "gay, lesbian, or homosexual" in the Yankelovich 1993 population study sample.

Yankelovich researchers monitor approximately fifty different social values among research participants from year to year. They then follow and interpret what these social values and their fluctuations can mean in relationship to the consumer's ideas and behaviors.

The following is a review of what Yankelovich researchers were able to discern about gay and lesbian Americans, their views, their ideas, and how they differ from the overall, predominantly heterosexual population.

Understanding the Data: Statistical Significance

Differences between the gay/lesbian population and the general population that are statistically significant at the 95 percent confidence level will be boxed in each illustrated chart as follows (a detailed analysis of the Yankelovich methodology is explained in the Appendix):

- Positive differences are indicated by a clear box
- Negative differences have a shaded box
- Numbers that are not boxed do not represent statistically significant differences from the general population. That is to say, differences observed could have occurred due to chance.

Population Size

As stated in Chapter 3, approximately 6 percent of the 1993 Yankelovich MONITOR's sample identified themselves as "gay/lesbian/

homosexual," a figure somewhere between the percentages reported in other studies (such as the Guttmacher Institute and the often-quoted-out-of-context Kinsey report and ranging from 1 percent to 10 percent, respectively).

Age and Sex

The gay/lesbian population mirrors the heterosexual population's distribution in the following characteristics:

	Gay/Lesbian %	Heterosexual %
Sex:		
Male	44	48
Female	56	52
Age:		
16-24	22	17
25-34	21	23
35-44	21	21
45-54	13	13
55-64	8	10
65+	15	16

Ethnicity

The gay/lesbian sample is evenly distributed throughout the population with regard to ethnicity, although there is a slightly above-average representation of Hispanics.

	Gay/Lesbian %	Heterosexual %
Race:		
White	72	78
African American	11	11
Spanish/Hispanic	13	8
Other Minority	4	3

Education

Level of educational attainment is significantly higher for the gay/lesbian sample, particularly at the graduate school level. This demographic distinction usually carries with it substantially higher income levels as well as employment at the professional/executive level; subsequent tables in this section of the report will show that this is—contrary to recent media misinformation—*not the case for the gay/lesbian population.*

	Gay/Lesbian %	Heterosexual %
Level of education attained by respondent:		
Less than 4 years of high school	20	26
High school graduate	31	37
Any college (net)	49	37
Less than 4 years	23	19
College graduate	12	11
Graduate school	14	7

Employment and Occupation

There were no significant differences in the broad demographic categories of employment and occupation, except that gays/lesbians are more likely to be self-employed. This fact is particularly worth noting since business-to-business marketing approaches aimed at gay and lesbian individuals is relatively nonexistent. Many opportunities to reach gay and lesbian businesspeople exist through business and trade organizations and business publications and newsletters.

	Gay/Lesbian %	Heterosexual %
Employed (net):	62	62
Part time	15	13
Full time	47	49
Self-employed	18	11
Occupation:		
White-collar professional, executive, managerial	16	18
White collar other	22	18
Blue collar	27	29

Income

Income among the American gay/lesbian population as a whole is slightly lower than that of the heterosexual population. This finding contradicts a popular myth about the relative affluence of American lesbians and gay men, one that is often based on comparisons between general population data and data collected by the sales and marketing departments of gay and lesbian publications whose readers, by definition, are not representative of the mainstream of all gay consumers.

A more reliable and valid comparison of income is presented in the following tables, using data that compares the general population of gays/lesbians to the general population of heterosexuals.

Overall income is slightly lower for the gay/lesbian group as a whole, a difference that is driven primarily by the slightly lower earnings of gay men compared to the heterosexual group.

While it is true that some dual-income-earning, predominantly white, gay male households have incomes much greater than the national average, overall gay males had lower personal and household incomes than their heterosexual counterparts. However, no substantial difference in income distribution exists between lesbians and heterosexual females; in both cases, female income is below that of males. This observation is especially compelling since discrimination toward women as a group may be more widespread regardless of race or sexual orientation than previously thought. Certainly much has been written about the economic subjugation of women, but this specific area stands out as one suggesting that more research is warranted.

Lee Badgett's work at the University of Maryland's School of Public Affairs is particularly worth noting again. Badgett found that gay and bisexual men earn from 9.5 to 25.9 percent less than straight men, and that lesbian and bisexual women face a sexual orientation penalty (meaning they fare less well when their "gayness" is known) ranging from 13.1 to 14.8 percent, which drops to only 5 percent when taking occupation into account.[11]

Income Differences Between the Sexes
(Gay/Lesbian and Heterosexual)

	Gay Male (63) %	Hetero-sexual Male (1145) %	Lesbian (80) %	Hetero-sexual Female (1215) %
Personal income:				
Under $25K	81	65	87	88
$25-$49,999	13	29	11	11
$50-$99,999	3	5	1	1
$100K+	3	1	*	*
Household income:				
Under $25K	37	32	47	43
$25-$49,999	49	42	33	37
$50-$99,999	9	23	18	17
$100K+	5	3	2	3
Mean personal income (000)	$21.5	$22.5	$13.3	$13.2
Mean household income (000)	$37.4	$39.3	$34.8	$34.4
Mean household size	3.03	3.05	2.78	2.97

*Less than 0.5%.

Marital Status

Forty-two percent of the gay/lesbian population report that they are married. While the sex of the spouse is not specified, the fact remains that more than one opinion may often contribute to any given household buying decision. This may have significant implications for marketers.

	Gay/Lesbian %	Heterosexual %
Currently:		
Married	42	54
Never married	44	26

Parental Status

While gay men are less than half as likely as heterosexual males to be fathers, lesbians are nearly as likely to be mothers as their heterosexual counterparts. One half of the gay/lesbian sample are parents, and one quarter live in households with children under eighteen present. Consequently, many products related to parenting are relevant to this segment of gay/lesbian parents.

	Gay/Lesbian %	Heterosexual %
Parents	50	66
Among women	67	72
Among men	27	60
Children (under 18) in household		
Among women	32	36
Among men	15	28
Mean household size	2.89	3.01

Religious Affiliation

Gays/lesbians are less likely to report Protestant religious affiliation. This is especially true of the Baptists and may agree with the lower representation of this population in the South (Baptists are more concentrated in the South). There were no other significant differences found in this area.

	Gay/Lesbian %	Heterosexual %
Religious affiliation:		
Protestant (net)	46	56
Baptist	17	27
Churches of Christ	1	3
Disciples of Christ	3	1
Episcopal	6	2
Lutheran	10	6
Methodist	3	8
Presbyterian	2	3
United Church of Christ	1	2
Latter Day Saints/Mormon	*	2
Other Protestant	3	5
Roman Catholic	25	22
Jewish	4	2
Eastern Orthodox	1	1
Unitarian	1	1
Other religion	6	8
None	12	10

*Less than 0.5%.

Political Affiliation

In what is sure to be a controversial and perhaps contested area of fact, the Yankelovich data confirms what some have long believed but have been unable to confirm: that gay and lesbian Americans are more likely to be Republican than previously thought.

Even with the heterosexual population, there has been a widely held belief that the gay/lesbian population is decidedly Democratic, but Yankelovich MONITOR data indicate that the gay and lesbian population is no different from its heterosexual counterpart when it comes to the matter of political affiliation. A higher proportion of gays/lesbians do, however, report a liberal political point of view.

	Gay/Lesbian %	Heterosexual %
Political affiliation:		
Democrat	45	44
Republican	27	26
Independent	21	22
Other	7	8
Political point of view:		
Conservative	34	40
Moderate	37	41
Liberal	28	17
Radical	1	2

ATTITUDINAL PROFILE
OF GAY AND LESBIAN AMERICANS

Yankelovich revealed five key areas of significant difference between the gay/lesbian and the heterosexual populations. Topic areas of difference were grouped into subjects of significant interest.

- Individuality and self-understanding
- Social interaction
- Experiencing life's diversity
- Maintaining independence
- Skepticism and self-protection

Key Areas of Difference: Individuality and Self-Understanding

	Gay/Lesbian %	Heterosexual %
Strong support for trend:		
Introspection (need for self-understanding)	43	23
Mind-Body (commitment to maximizing health and energy)	44	30
Presence (commitment to maximizing physical appearance)	53	42

The gay/lesbian sample appears to be more concerned than the heterosexual population about understanding themselves and their motivations. This is marked by a particularly strong need for self-understanding, which is evident in the data, as well as the interesting notion that many gays/lesbians believe themselves to possess a higher IQ than most, though many feel somewhat alienated from mainstream America. This group's heightened interest in optimizing physical condition and appearance is also very clear.

Yankelovich researchers focused further examination of the data in relationship to individual appearance and style and drew the conclusion that there is a stronger interest among gay and lesbian Americans in keeping up with "the latest" in fashion. While this may not be new information to many, the heightened interest in physical appearance in combination with other social issues previously discussed draws our attention to issues of self-esteem within the gay and lesbian sample; either less of it, or perhaps a heightened sense of it.

What could be some possible explanations for these interests?

- Increased attention to appearance is a nonverbal communication, affirming gay and lesbian personal good health and strong character
- A need to fit into a perceived standard within a local gay/lesbian community
- A desire to differentiate one's self in a way separate from or more acceptable to heterosexual society
- Perhaps an overcompensating response to a perceived covert discrimination by heterosexuals

Key Areas of Difference: Social Interaction and Experiencing Life's Diversity

Companies marketing products that are related to the following list, take note. The gay/lesbian population is clearly and actively looking for new products and services across the board.

	Gay/Lesbian %	Heterosexual %
Looking for new:		
Places to go out with friends	52	42
Foods to eat at home	49	37
Discount stores	30	23
Department stores	29	18
Magazines	26	19
Fast food restaurants	22	15
Home entertainment devices	19	15
Mail order catalogs	15	9

Key Areas of Difference: Maintaining Independence

	Gay/Lesbian %	Heterosexual %
Strong support for trend:		
Need for Control (need to maximize personal control of life)	46	35
Away from Clutter and Complexity (need to eliminate nonessentials)	24	15
Accommodation to Technology (need to feel comfortable with technology)	47	33

Analysis of the data indicates that gays/lesbians perceive a high level of stress in their lives; they appear to feel pressure on all fronts. Only 2 percent of the sample state that they do not feel that they are under stress (compared to 11 percent of the heterosexual population). This stress is manifested in a number of buying behaviors such as a higher level of interest in and consumption of leisure vacations. Sustained feelings of stress appear to lead to a strong need to achieve greater control and certainty in life. Times are not certain and planning for the future is difficult. Frustrated attempts to gain more control become yet another source of stress for this population.

Eighty-five percent of gay males and lesbians feel the need to find ways of reducing stress in their lives. This is a significantly high number compared to the heterosexual population. While the ability to remove stress from people's lives may be beyond the scope of marketing, the data indicate an opportunity to add value for the gay/lesbian consumer by streamlining stress out of the product or the purchase decision process.

	Gay/Lesbian %	Heterosexual %
Total agree:		
Feel the need to find ways of reducing stress in my life	85	78

Key Areas of Difference: Skepticism and Self-Protection

	Gay/Lesbian %	Heterosexual %
Strong support for trend:		
Anti-Bigness ("big" companies are the consumer's enemy)	35	26
Victimization (outside forces are seeking to harm me)	29	20

A feeling that "the world is against me," and that "there is no one I can trust" is apparent in the responses of this group. The data indicate a low level of trust in institutions such as government and business and the clear sense that the only trustworthy person or institution is one's self.

THE PSYCHOLOGY OF DISENFRANCHISEMENT

The "Psychology of disenfranchisement" is based on the ideas of Yankelovich researcher Rex Briggs.

There are three components that drive the psychology of disenfranchisement: alienation, cynicism, and perceived victimization. These components interact with and intensify each other.

Alienation

Alienation is one of the most important components of the psychology of disenfranchisement, and may be due to negative perceptions, stereotypes, and discrimination condoned and practiced by the dominant culture. The perception of separation from the mainstream culture can create severe stress and can be considered the impetus for the psychology of disenfranchisement.

	Gay/Lesbian %	Heterosexual %
Total agree:		
My personal values and point of view are not shared by most Americans today	40	31
Sometimes I have to compromise my principles	76	65
Describes me:		
Different from others	55	27
A loner	36	13
Outside the mainstream	24	10

Cynicism

Cynicism is one of the inevitable offshoots of alienation, and results in the conviction that things will go wrong, that harm is to be expected, and that the only thing that can be trusted is the propensity of things to happen badly. It involves a sense that the institutions of society (from which one is alienated) are not only remote, but inimical.

	Gay/Lesbian %	Heterosexual %
Total agree:		
With minor exceptions, the honesty and integrity of business in its dealings with the public is at a very high level	37	46
If the opportunity arises, most businesses will take advantage of the public if they feel they are not likely to be found out	63	54

Victimization

Victimization is a feeling that develops out of the perception of intentional or unintentional undeserved mistreatment by other individuals, organizations, or institutions. Victimization is a logical outgrowth of feelings of cynicism and alienation from the dominant culture.

	Gay/Lesbian %	Heterosexual %
Strong support for trend:		
Victimization	29	20

Over time, this cycle can become entrenched. The perceived victimization legitimizes and justifies cynicism in one's mind. The lack of trust fostered by a cynical perspective thereby increases the original feelings of alienation.

The intensity of the feelings of disenfranchisement should be thought of as lying on a continuum stretching from the endpoints of complete enfranchisement to complete disenfranchisement. Few are at either extreme. But all affect the producer-consumer dynamic—especially in relation to gays and lesbians.

Communication from Dominant Culture		Interpretation by Disenfranchised Individual
Malice intended	⇨	Victimization perceived
No malice intended	⇨	Victimization perceived (misinterpreted)
Malice intended	⇨	*No* victimization perceived (misinterpreted)
No malice intended	⇨	*No* victimization perceived

BUSINESS AND MARKETING IMPLICATIONS

Communications that focus on serving any of the aforementioned needs are likely to strike a chord with the gay male or lesbian consumer and encourage a purchase. A marketer can offset the negative effects of the cycle of disenfranchisement and build a valuable relationship in several ways:

- Develop, print, and circulate an employment hiring policy prohibiting discrimination based on sexual orientation in all areas of the workplace.
- Communicate this information in press releases and company-wide memos.
- Install domestic partner health care insurance for gay and lesbian employees or make compensation arrangements in their absence.
- Focus on inclusion of gays/lesbians in the consumer family (offsets alienation).
- Identify cultural reference points to which gays/lesbians can relate. Avoid stereotypes.
- Develop honest and consistent messages related to product offerings (to minimize cynicism).
- Underpromise and overdeliver (to minimize victimization).
- Communicate respect for the consumer.
- When something does go wrong, do more than just fix it (defuses cynicism, relieves feelings of victimization).
- Listen patiently and attentively to complaints.
- Accept blame.
- Fix the problem.
- Provide additional compensation.
- Reduce stress.
- Streamline stress out of the purchase process.
- Offer opportunities for self-indulgence.

The overriding point for marketers, however, is that many gay males and lesbians view the world through a prism of cynicism toward business, are quick to interpret actions as attempts at victimization, and feel alienated from the dominant culture. Marketing and communication strategies that take into consideration the influence of these factors can sidestep the pitfalls and leverage the benefits of their management approaches and product or service offerings, and thus increase the success of their business, management, and consumer market planning. And as has been established, genuinely seeking to accommodate gay and lesbian consumers in the workplace as well as the marketplace positions a company as being "more socially conscious," thereby buttressing brand loyalty among heterosexual consumers as well.

As lesbian and gay culture has become more visible in mainstream media, so have the covers of lesbian and gay magazines become more "mainstream-looking" in an effort to tap into important advertising dollars. (Covers from *Curve* and *OUT* magazines reprinted with permission of the publishers. *The Advocate* cover published with permission of *The Advocate*, issue 769, ⒸⒸ copyright Liberation Publications, Inc., 1998.

The beach "kiss" has been the mainstay of heterosexual advertisements since the 1950s and is now recreated by Olivia in this new benchmark of lesbian consumer marketing.

By playing on a theme from the American war years, Diesel has formulated for gay men the same iconography that Olivia has developed for lesbians.

Since the early ACT UP years, Miller Beer has become a visible part of the national gay and lesbian advertising community's support network—both in their treatment of marketing campaigns and in their support of nonprofit fund-raising.

Great target marketing on behalf of AT&T. A well-utilized play on the word *true* as a pun that serves to communicate inclusiveness in many different ways while also educating the consumer about the product's benefits.

Focusing on just how versatile American Express Travelers Cheques really are serves as a way to position not only the product but the entire company as inclusive, contemporary, and innovative. This ad appeared in *OUT* magazine; note the two female signatories.

This leading commercial was a first in television advertising. It communicated inclusiveness across a broad range of consumer groups while allowing gay men to be seen as everyday people. If IKEA's next commercial includes lesbians, their competitors will really have their work cut out for them.

A strong advertising communication that speaks to many different demographic groups of women, regardless of income, race, or sexual orientation.

This shows how a company can position a product to gay and lesbian consumers while also communicating inclusiveness to all consumer groups. It's clean, brand-focused, and matter-of-fact.

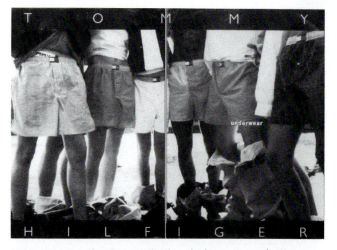

Whimsical, unoffending production design communicates many different things to many different groups of men, especially the importance of having a sense of individuality.

A pioneering example of same-sex imagery that communicates a sense of warmth and "matter-of-factness" about a new product of particular interest to gay male consumers.

Carefully produced and strategically placed Marlboro billboards have long appeared in neighborhoods across America where gay as well as straight consumers will easily notice their presence.

The magazine known for communicating a cutting-edge sense of glamour attained new heights of respectability with gay and lesbian consumers by producing this very witty, tongue-in-cheek cover that got lots of attention in the media and in many different social circles.

There was a time when *The New Yorker* would not have acknowledged this level of verisimilitude (or even satire) when it comes to gay visibility. The magazine has clearly incorporated an understanding of the gay and lesbian consumer since Tina Brown's installation as editor in chief, and her lead in making more editorial space for gay- and lesbian-themed articles has been well received.

Mainstream America first began to accept the truth about AIDS and the importance of gay and lesbian culture in the early 1980s. However, noticeable advertising and editorial imagery—both about and aimed at gay and lesbian consumers on a regular basis—did not begin to appear widely in the national media until the 1990s.

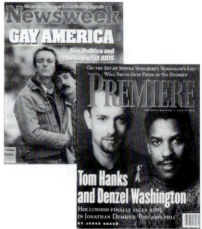

Being gay, HIV positive, and a celebrity is now part of mainstream American advertising and media imagery.

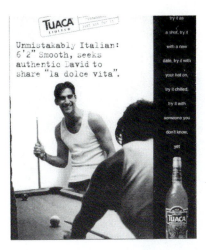

Unmistakably Italian:
6'2" Smooth, seeks
authentic David to
share "la dolce vita".

A strong state-of-the-art example of well-crafted advertising that communicates same-sex attraction and a sense of realness about gay male culture. Everything is on cue, from the wardrobe choice to the game being played.

Benetton has mastered the art of communicating diversity to a broad range of consumers on a broad range of social issues. Everything has been tackled, from war and the environment to HIV, condom use, American democracy, and the politics of sexual identity.

Placing Martina Navratilova next to wide receiver Art Monk is brilliant because it directly communicates diversity across a broad consumer demographic spectrum: sports enthusiasts (whether they are men or women), racial minorities, and gay as well as straight consumers.

Companies that provide exclusive products to gay men and lesbians and then follow up by sharing some of their profits with the gay community will always be seen as the leaders.

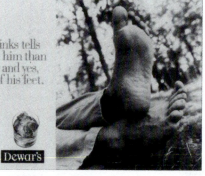

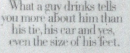

Gay and lesbian consumers will always appreciate the witty and the sassy. Dewar's has clearly found a way to tease everyone by intimating what is usually forbidden discussion among polite company.

Spectacular representation of dual messaging to straight and gay men. It communicates a clear and believable sense of company friendliness and trustworthiness.

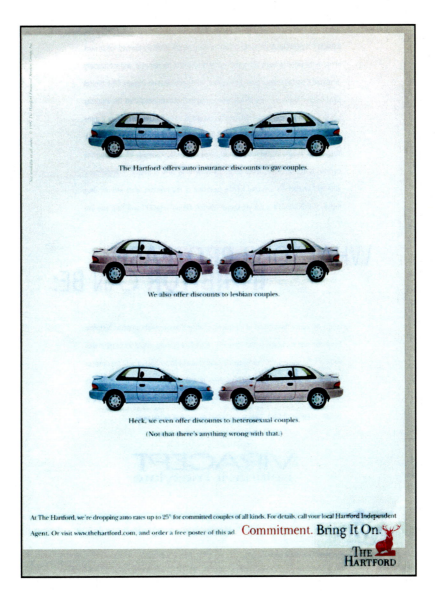

Source: Reprinted by permission of The Hartford Corporation.

Source: *OUT* magazine. Reprinted by permission of Anheuser-Busch.

Source: Reprinted by permission of Do Tell Inc., The Rainbow Card.

Ted is making Steve supper.

Ted told Steve he was a race car driver.
Ted told Steve he was rich.
Steve told Ted to try another approach.
So tonight, he is making Steve supper.
Uh oh!
Steve wants something healthy *and* tasty.
He wants **the impossible!**
Ted fixes him a Gardenburger.

Yum!

Look at Steve smile.
Who needs an expensive car
when you're a genius?

Gardenburger. Eating good just got great.

Chapter 5

Brand Loyalty, Management, and the Creative Process: Promoting Products and Services to Gay and Lesbian Consumers

You can't fake a Corporate Soul; either you have one or you'd better create one, fast.

Faith Popcorn, 1991[1]

The most important issue related to gay and lesbian target marketing is corporate workplace policy.

Many companies refer to the Equality Project's Equality Principles on Sexual Orientation for direction on how best to implement and address gay- and lesbian-specific issues when formulating or updating corporate guidelines. The Equality Project is a nonprofit organization founded by gay and lesbian citizens active in American corporate, labor, and socially responsible investment circles.

A serious analysis of how your company stands according to these guidelines as formulated by the Equality Project would be well advised before initiating any gay or lesbian marketing campaign.

THE EQUALITY PRINCIPLES ON SEXUAL ORIENTATION

1. Explicit prohibitions against discrimination based on sexual orientation are included in the company's written employment policy statement.

2. Discrimination against HIV-positive employees or those with AIDS is strictly prohibited.
3. Employee groups, regardless of sexual orientation, are given equal standing with other employee associations.
4. Diversity training is inclusive of sexual orientation issues.
5. Spousal benefits are offered to domestic partners of employees, regardless of sexual orientation, on an equal basis with those granted to married employees.
6. Company advertising policy bars the use of negative sexual orientation stereotypes in media communications.
7. The company does not discriminate in the sale and purchase of goods and services on the basis of sexual orientation.
8. Written nondiscrimination policies on sexual orientation are disseminated throughout the company. A senior company official monitors compliance companywide.[2]

Corporate Policy

At a minimum, a company conducting business with gay and lesbian consumers must have a nondiscrimination policy statement that includes the words "sexual orientation." For some companies, all that is required is the simple insertion of the two words "sexual" and "orientation" into the existing policy. Of course, a company's legal counsel should be consulted regarding the addition of these words and the grandfathering of a nondiscriminatory policy companywide.

If your company does not have a policy, immediately establish one or begin lobbying the right people to get one installed. Companies that target gay and lesbian consumers without having first taken this step leave themselves and their employees vulnerable to a multitude of harassment lawsuits and potential public relations challenges down the road—particularly if an advertising campaign aimed at gay consumers does well, but the press later learns that the company's official policy on sexual orientation is lacking or nonexistent.

Corporate Action

Publicly back up the corporate policy of not discriminating based on sexual orientation by supporting or contributing in-kind services to organizations that defend gay and lesbian human rights or support community cohesion. This contribution should be in addition to any support of AIDS-related causes. AIDS-related contributions alone do not count in the minds of some gay and lesbian consumers as necessarily being "human-rights" oriented contributions.

Every city in the United States with a population of 250,000 or more has some kind of gay or lesbian organization or is within driving distance of a larger city that does. Marketers and the companies they serve simply cannot afford to be perceived by a single gay or lesbian consumer as exploitive or on a mission to "profit off of them."

Besides, too many companies sooner or later find themselves in a position where they have to take a stand on some community, industry, or political issue of importance to their customers. It pays to be—and to have been all along—on the official side of a company's customers.

Local gay and lesbian organizations provide one of the easiest ways for a company to align itself with the community—the very people with which it is seeking to do business. Clarence Patton, program coordinator with Empire State Pride Agenda, a gay and lesbian political action committee in New York, sees gay and lesbian organizations as the principal "watchdogs [who are] creating visibility. Their mission is to improve the quality of life of lesbian and gay people." Paula Ettelbrick, legislative counsel for Empire State Pride Agenda agrees, stating, "When we are invisible, our very existence can be denied."

Marketers to gays and lesbians must remain mindful of this constant: nearly every gay and lesbian organization in the United States is ultimately fighting for the same thing in their lobbying and activism efforts for equal rights and protection under the law—visibility and a better quality of life for all gay and lesbian Americans. Different groups certainly focus on different aspects of gay and lesbian emancipation, but all are committed to improving gay and lesbian quality of life and creating visibility. And business cannot go wrong by getting behind a local or national effort accordingly.

It's simple. It's cost effective. Do it. Support gay and lesbian philanthropy, and find ways to make your support known to your employees and your customers. It's common sense. It also makes competitive sense.

Market Research

Conducting extensive research prior to the launch of any advertising campaign aimed at gay and lesbian consumers is elementary marketing logic.

Treat the research process with the same level of sophistication, importance, and budget allowance as any other market research project within the company. Make sure copywriters, art directors, and brand managers ask themselves questions about how the product or service might be communicated differently based on issues of sexual orientation.

There simply may be no differences or requirements for customized messaging. Or, there may be several factors:

- What are the general gay and lesbian demographics?
- Are they different from your general (heterosexual) demographics?
- Does race play a factor in association with sexual orientation?
- Were the demographics obtained using statistically relevant sampling techniques?
- What exact age group are you targeting?
- Is your message mindful of women?
- Is your message mindful of gay or lesbian parents?
- What income category?
- How many are single or in committed relationships?
- What assumptions are you making that are not founded in research?
- Are any gays or lesbians associated with your advertising project?

Make every attempt to produce some kind of testing campaign or run a focus group including gay and lesbian and heterosexual participants. Ideally, focus groups with gay and lesbian consumers should be conducted by gay or lesbian moderators who make their own sexual orientation known to the participants.

If the budget allows, marketing materials intended to attract gay and lesbian consumers should also be cross-tested against focus groups composed exclusively of heterosexuals. It is important to gauge how the bulk of a company's current consumers might react to the creative tone you have taken in targeting gay- or lesbian-specific audiences and vice versa.

Focus groups composed exclusively of gay and lesbian participants always yield surprising and useful insights that can be applied to an entire range of concerns within a company's marketing strategy.

Research, research, research. It pays. Allocate money to gay and lesbian focus groups or market testing. Companies serious about targeting gay and lesbian consumers can't afford not to.

Community Involvement

For smaller companies, this is a particularly important area. One of the easiest ways to go about launching a gay- and lesbian-oriented advertising campaign in small to mid-sized cities is to simply consult with a company's current gay and lesbian employees or with the gay and lesbian business community in a given company's principal area of economic activity.

Some of the best marketing ideas and concepts come from administrative support staffs, traffic departments, and proofreading pools. Circulate office memos about the decision to target gay and lesbian consumers and encourage employees to attend brainstorming sessions. The results are always surprising and the degree of good will fostered within a company's labor force is immeasurable. Moreover, every major American city now has writers, art directors, and in some cases entire advertising agencies that specialize in gay- and lesbian-oriented marketing and research. Even in America's smaller and mid-sized cities, a business can always turn to the advertising department of the local gay and lesbian newspaper and usually obtain competent and cost effective advertising and marketing advice.

But the point still stands—for both large and small companies: conduct research first; facts always matter.

Competent and shrewd marketers seeking to target gay and lesbian consumers in American business regularly utilize, customize, and combine these four areas of focus with existing knowledge about the company's products and services.

The end result is always a cunning and powerful advertising campaign that wins gay and lesbian customers and instills broadscale goodwill within a company. Be resourceful, be inclusive. It will be apparent in the marketing campaign.

TAKE ACTION; BE DECISIVE

Once you have examined your company's policies in relation to the Equality Project's Equality Principles, and have considered the above four areas, it is time to take action.

Be decisive. Don't backtrack or "tone down" a campaign to appease an uncomfortable manager unless the research indicates a subtle message is required.

Gay and lesbian consumers are very skeptical. They have extremely well-calibrated cow pie detectors. A campaign that has had too many hands in it for too long will always come off looking contrived, forced, too clean, too "safe," or simply dull.

A word of caution: Each person brings his or her own insights, prejudices, and insecurities into every decision-making process—particularly when it comes to sensitive creative undertakings such as the development of gay and lesbian marketing campaigns.

Too many chiefs bring down the tepee. Once everyone's opinion has been consulted, once the research analysis has come in, take action. Vacillating can send the wrong message to gay and lesbian employees.

FIFTY GREAT WAYS TO BUILD STRONGER CUSTOMER RELATIONS WITH GAY AND LESBIAN CONSUMERS

Here is a summary of fifty ways to better position your company and its products to appeal to gay and lesbian consumers. Following this list is additional information on boycotts and backlash issues, as well as personal opinions and insights from community leaders and corporate representatives, on matters of race, gender, and class—in relation to sexual orientation.

1. Install and conspicuously post a companywide policy statement barring discrimination against employees, vendors, and
   independent contractors based on sexual orientation. Include
   this information in a company letter to new employees and
   vendors. Annually circulate along with payroll checks the
   company's policy statement barring discrimination based on
   sexual orientation. Print statements of this policy and insert
   them periodically with company check payments to creditors
   or donations to local charity groups.

2. Organize, support, or make clear your company's willingness
   to support gay and lesbian philanthropy in the community as
   well as employee organizations within the company based on
   sexual orientation. Give the same level of support in writing,
   spirit, and action to gay and lesbian employee groups as you
   give to all other employee-centered activity clubs and affinity
   organizations.

3. Advertise in gay- or lesbian-owned publications. Make known
   to your newspaper or advertising account executive that your
   company has an interest in conducting cooperative advertising
   or marketing-related programs in association with nonprofit
   organizations.

4. Provide domestic partnership benefits or their monetary
   equivalent to your gay and lesbian employees. Consult with
   the National Gay and Lesbian Task Force or Human Rights
   Campaign in Washington on how to go about creating domestic partnership benefits in your company.

5. Obtain quality gay and lesbian mailing lists when planning
   direct mail or telemarketing campaigns to new customers.
   Consult with gay newspaper advertising representatives and
   development directors at gay and lesbian nonprofit organizations on where to obtain good gay and lesbian mailing lists.
   Contact the Gay and Lesbian Alliance Against Defamation
   on guidelines for producing affirmative, nondefaming advertising communications.

6. Consider placing occasional progay- or lesbian-identified advertisements in nongay publications when matters of equal
   rights come up in the state where your company's home office
   is located. The attention garners lots of free press and the

goodwill fostered among straight as well as gay and lesbian consumers is immeasurable. It also communicates to nongay customers your company's level of commitment to fairness and integrity in business and customer relations regardless of partisan politics.

7. Routinely advertise job opportunities in gay and lesbian newspapers. Include in the advertising copy information that your company is an equal opportunity employer with a written policy barring discrimination based on sexual orientation. Include this information in job postings in nongay publications as well.

8. Communicate your company's official support of ENDA, the federal Employment Non-Discrimination Act. Contact the Human Rights Campaign in Washington for complete, updated information on ENDA.

9. Include national and local area gay and lesbian publication's on routine distribution lists of press releases that communicate important public information about your company.

10. Promote and support diversity education on the job and in the community that includes information about AIDS and HIV. Place periodic classified advertisements in gay and lesbian publications drawing attention to your company's policy in this regard.

11. Support your local gay and lesbian community center or create a fund drive to establish one.

12. When it comes to promoting your products and services to straight as well as gay and lesbian customers, it's always best to underpromise in your general marketing and advertising communications to the public at large; but overdeliver when it comes to providing the actual products and customer services to customers. Send overnight replacement products in place of those previously delivered damaged. Offer gift certificates to unhappy customers.

13. Make contributions to local women's halfway houses.

14. Include information about homophobia in diversity education training in the workplace.

15. Be sure to use sexually inclusive language (e.g., partner, lover) in marketing communications when referring to romantic and spousal relationships.
16. Be sure to use shrewd, sexually inclusive imagery in advertising photography and marketing graphics (e.g., capturing appropriate same-sex affection that could be construed as being either romantic or merely friendship).
17. Lend the company name in speaking out against hate and violence of all kinds. Insist that language be included that identifies the importance of protecting gays and lesbians in this regard.
18. Make sure your personnel director or human resources administrator has a copy of *Straight Talk About Gays in the Workplace* by Liz Winfeld and Sue Spielman.[3]
19. When public relations or customer service mistakes happen, accept blame publicly. Do more than necessary to fix the problem immediately. Offer immediate compensation to unhappy customers. Include a copy of the company's antidiscrimination statement with your customer service letter of apology.
20. Make an annual contribution to the Hetrick Martin Institute in Manhattan and the Lesbian Herstory Archives in Brooklyn, New York. They are two of the most important organizations in the country when it comes to gay and lesbian youth issues and important archives on exclusively lesbian material.
21. Confront sexist or antigay humor in the workplace. Communicate that homophobia is more than a word; in society it translates and manifests itself as hatred and fear based on ignorance.
22. Whenever controversy surfaces in relation to personnel issues in your industry, consider issuing simple policy statements to the press calling attention to your company's support of basic human rights as they pertain to gay- and lesbian-related issues.
23. Include organizations that support gay and lesbian community development efforts on your company's annual charitable giving list or employee matching funds programs. Be sure to circulate this information to employees and stockholders as well.
24. Make complimentary product or service contributions available to volunteers at local nonprofit organizations.

25. Give away free samples of your company's products or gift certificates for your services at gay pride celebrations, parades, and festivals.

26. Form alliances with community organizations and other companies that acknowledge and support sexual diversity in the workplace and the marketplace. Start by attending fund-raisers, benefits, and dinners where these issues are a focus.

27. Consider the benefits and ramifications of supporting or not supporting gun control legislation at the local and national level.

28. Create relationship marketing links on your company's cyberspace home page to gay and lesbian Web sites. Incorporate contests for prizes connected to gay or lesbian magazine subscriptions, and gay-owned company products and services.

29. Draw attention to your company's logo and good name by sponsoring periodic public information advertisements in gay and lesbian publications about issues of importance to gay and straight people alike (e.g., health care, child welfare, etc.).

30. Support the Lambda Legal Defense Fund in Washington, DC.

31. Circulate memos prior to companywide events encouraging employees to bring their spouses, partners, or significant others to official events and activities.

32. Send a representative from your company to the annual Creating Change and Out and Equal conferences sponsored by the National Gay and Lesbian Task Force.

33. Include the words "domestic partner" in advertising copy, direct mail copy, and as a choice on all company forms, applications, and registrations.

34. Form strategic alliances with local business organizations that share your company's philosophy of gay and lesbian inclusivity in the workplace and marketplace.

35. Provide local soup kitchen volunteers with complimentary tickets from your company on a first-come, first-serve basis to gay- and non-gay-related events in the community.

36. Advertise in theater and concert programs highlighting gay-related content or subject matter.

37. Include statements in marketing copy and direct mail communications that your company does not discriminate based on sexual orientation.
38. Compare how inclusive your company is with other businesses by reading *The 100 Best Companies for Gay Men and Lesbians* by Ed Mickens, or *Cracking the Corporate Closet* by Sean Strub, Dan Baker, and Bill Henning.[4]
39. When planning marketing campaigns and strategies, consider what specifically separates you from your competitors in ways that may appeal to gay and lesbian consumers. Does geography, weather, or local social custom affect your marketing plans? What holiday, social, or calendar activities might coincide with the nature of your products and services? What annual gay and lesbian community activities occur that may provide marketing opportunities for your company?
40. In communicating information about your products or services, focus on how they make life easier for your gay or lesbian consumers.
41. Instruct your advertising agency to communicate your company's support of individuality and creativity in advertising and marketing communications. Ask how they are reaching your gay and lesbian customers. Insist that your agency of record include gay and lesbian participants in focus-group testing.
42. Support PFLAG (Parents and Friends of Lesbians and Gays).
43. Cosponsor raffles and sweepstakes with local gay- and lesbian-owned businesses.
44. Cross-promote your products and services in association with other companies that maintain good relations with gay and lesbian consumers.
45. Participate conspicuously in health-related fund-raisers such as breast cancer research and birth defects in addition to those your company supports in the fight against AIDS.
46. Be sure to include gay-friendly language in marketing surveys about lifestyle issues related to your products and services (e.g., partner, significant other, or domestic partner).
47. Place a copy of Annette Friskopp and Sharon Silverstein's *Straight Jobs, Gay Lives* in the company library.[5]

48. Encourage gay and lesbian employees to utilize a personal holiday on the Friday before or the Monday after Gay Pride Weekend celebrations.
49. Run public relations advertisements on behalf of your company in both gay and nongay publications supporting gay and lesbian pride in America during gay pride month (June).
50. Encourage management to be good-natured—even participatory—about cross-dressing at the office on October 31st.

CORPORATE NIGHTMARES: THE TRUTH ABOUT BOYCOTTS AND BACKLASH

The gay and lesbian community cannot be bought. But it can be engaged through sound business and marketing practices that result in social change.

Companies that have attempted to thwart social change in relation to gays and lesbians or have behaved indifferently at politically sensitive times have usually been the companies that have had to deal with backlash and boycotts.

Interestingly, though, the most costly backlashes have actually come from within the gay and lesbian community—usually brought on by companies that have not maintained a decent relationship with them as consumers; not from Christian fundamentalists refusing to buy a brand of detergent because a prime-time television show introduced a gay character.

There are cases of such occurrences, however. Numerous sponsors refused to advertise on an early 1990s episode of *thirtysomething* that portrayed two gay male characters having a conversation in bed. Unfortunately for the fundamentalists, that news came and went in about a week.

Since that time, numerous gay and lesbian characters have been introduced on television sitcoms and dramas during prime-time viewing hours with no backlash. Ellen coming out, Roseanne's famous lesbian kiss episode, and other gay-oriented plots actually increased ratings and market share at the time, as did the Barbra Streisand NBC production starring Glenn Close in *The Margarethe Cammermeyer Story*, a true account of a gay woman who was discharged from the U.S. military.

Boycotts were most popular during the 1960s when various groups began picketing and raising public attention about companies that were supplying materials for the U.S. military during the Vietnam War.

It was at this time that "the phenomenon of socially responsible investing probably originated," writes Ed Mickens in *The Advocate*.[6] Mickens further comments that in the 1970s stockholder actions and boycotts "became popular as a way to put the economic squeeze on the apartheid government of South Africa. . . ." The tactic or its threat worked, at least in the sense that most American companies withdrew from South Africa.

The first shareholder resolution against Cracker Barrel was in April 1994 and was sponsored by the New York City Comptroller's office. It sought the reinstatement of fired gay and lesbian employees and recommended the adoption of a nondiscrimination policy based on sexual orientation. It garnered over 15 percent of the vote among shareholders of Cracker Barrel stock in 1994 and about the same again in 1995, according to Dianne Bratcher, co-chair at the time of the Wall Street Project (an organization of gay and lesbian shareholder activists), which helped lead the fight. To date the action has not resulted in the implementation of a nondiscrimination policy statement, but Cracker Barrel's stock, which grew enormously between 1988 and 1992, has remained largely unchanged since its troubles with gay and lesbian consumers began.

Whether Cracker Barrel's stock price is tied to its policies is not known. But as gay and lesbian consumers continue to organize and make their concerns known not only to government but to Wall Street, the real backlash threat that marketers and stockholders need to be aware of is the one that can erupt from within the gay and lesbian community itself. One of the most memorable gay and lesbian boycotts in American history was launched against the Florida Citrus Commission in 1977. It lasted over two years and was motivated directly by Anita Bryant's Save Our Children campaign, which had placed full-page advertisements in the *Miami Herald* claiming that recruitment of children was necessary for the survival and growth of homosexuality.[7]

The boycott led to Anita Bryant's contract not being renewed by the commission and her singing career suffering a permanent setback as well. Looking back, many now consider her campaign against gay and lesbian America as unnecessarily obsessive and bizarre. But Ms. Bryant's campaign was more in reaction to the flexing of gay and lesbian activist muscle at the local level. She had specifically embarked on a mission to repeal Dade County's gay and lesbian equal protection clause and ended up dragging the orange juice industry with her. Although it cannot be proven that juice sales suffered, the Florida Citrus Commission had to deal with a public relations nightmare.

One of the most memorable corporate fiascoes involves the marketing of Coors beer. Adolph Coors Company in Golden, Colorado, has attempted, relatively unsuccessfully, to target the gay and lesbian consumer ever since a boycott of their company erupted and gained national attention in the late 1970s.

The accusations were many, but most specifically that the company had performed lie detector tests on individuals seeking employment with Coors—allegedly including questions about sexual orientation—and that they had contributed money to Anita Bryant's antigay crusade.

An official boycott was launched on April 12, 1977 by the AFL-CIO in support of Brewery Workers Local 366, which was not rescinded until 1987. Coors denied all the accusations while proceeding to move swiftly in the public relations arena. Shortly after the boycott was called, Joe Coors himself was quoted in *The Nation* as saying, "I honestly see very little appropriate role for unions in this day and age," which arguably made matters worse.[8]

Since that time, the company's public image has been changed somewhat through an ongoing marketing and public relations effort that has included the placement of advertisements in the gay and lesbian press as well as sponsorship of gay and lesbian community events. But their past will always follow them in the eyes of older gay and lesbian consumers, who will never forget.

As Russ Bellant wrote in *The Coors Connection: How Coors Family Philanthropy Undermines Democratic Pluralism,* "A number of affidavits, sworn testimony before the Senate, and press reports indicate that Coors did indeed use the polygraph to impose its narrow political views and quest for sexual conformity upon workers."[9] Coors has contributed hundreds of thousands of dollars to various gay, lesbian, and AIDS-related groups. They have also placed high-profile advertising in gay and lesbian publications.

The fact remains, though, that despite Coors' changes both in management and marketing decision making regarding gay and lesbian consumers, a majority of the company stock is still held by the Coors family. This fact is widely known among gay and lesbian consumers. So is the fact that the Coors family supports different conservative organizations including the Heritage Foundation and The Free Congress Foundation—both of which have routinely espoused public policies that would essentially deny gay and lesbian Americans their right to privacy and equal protection under the law if enacted.

Coors really has no choice but to continue its public relations and marketing campaign aimed at gay and lesbian consumers—if for no other reason than to protect its reputation among heterosexual consumers. Indeed it's hard to argue to the unknowing person on the street that Coors is a "homophobic company" if Coors advertising routinely shows up in gay and lesbian publications, and on the side of floats in gay and lesbian pride parades.

Buying advertising space in the gay and lesbian community may actually be money spent to buttress brand loyalty and identity among gay and lesbian consumers not old enough to know the history. Therein lies the next generation of Coors drinkers—and Coors must know that.

In 1990, a similar challenge was presented to Phillip Morris in relationship to its Miller Beer and Marlboro Cigarette brands. The company had been making contributions to Senator Jesse Helms, one of America's most outspoken antigay and antilesbian political leaders. Helms's position on AIDS research, funding, and prevention ideology was and continues to be unbelievably inhumane and counter to the goals not only of people living with HIV and AIDS, but the vast majority of gay and lesbian Americans, their families, and friends.

When information regarding the sheer size of the contributions Phillip Morris was making to Jesse Helms got out, AIDS activists (namely ACT UP) launched a high-profile and relatively successful boycott. In the end, Phillip Morris did not stop its funding of Senator Helms but it did agree to increase its funding to AIDS-related research (nearly doubling its contributions, which were already over a million dollars), which resulted in the boycott being called off by ACT UP. However, some older lesbians and gay men still will not drink Miller Beer because the company still has not taken steps to extend domestic partner health insurance to its gay employees.

Other boycotts and public demonstrations against major companies have received widespread attention, including those aimed at Burroughs Wellcome for their price-gouging of AZT medication to Americans living with HIV and AIDS, Cracker Barrel Old Country Store for firing and maintaining an official policy of not hiring gay and lesbian employees, and the state of Colorado for its attempted passage of Amendment 2—a law barring measures that protect lesbians and gay men against discrimination. At least seven Colorado municipalities passed such measures before they were ruled unconstitutional by the United States Supreme Court in 1996.

COMMON SENSE PUBLIC RELATIONS

Your company or the one you work for can learn from the mistakes of Coors, Phillip Morris, Cracker Barrel, and the state of Colorado. Corporate policy and corporate action in relationship to gay and lesbian consumers do, in fact, matter in modern America. And gay and lesbian consumers have made it clear that they are willing to boycott, conduct public demonstrations, and obtain public support for their grievances.

With each passing year, more and more mainstream companies rush to support the gay and lesbian community during America's annual gay pride and freedom day celebrations held each June. Each year, the political pressure on legislators increases as the press and electronic media present more accurate images of gay and lesbian Americans. The stakes get higher in the fight for equal rights for gays and lesbians. And each year gay and lesbian visibility grows. Another gay-themed movie gets released, another lesbian kiss makes its way onto prime-time television.

The issues related to gay and lesbian visibility, equal rights, equal protection under the law, and gay and lesbian market muscle are not going to go away. There will eventually be a federal statute barring discrimination against gay and lesbian individuals in housing, employment, and health care across the United States.

There is no sound reason for America's companies not to plan on getting on board with these issues ahead of time. It simply makes good marketing sense. It's also the right thing to do.

Corporate CEOs, presidents, vice presidents, senior-level managers, and public relations directors need to look at the companies they are working in and ask themselves if they can really afford to have one of their brands boycotted, debated, or dragged through the national press by gay and lesbian political leaders, AIDS activists, labor groups, and other human rights organizations.

The answer is no. It is never in the best interest of business to have to fight a boycott or negative press. As proven by the hits taken by the companies mentioned above, it is also exceedingly costly.

Good News

Good companies maintain good corporate policies. Very smart companies maintain very smart policies. They see that an ounce of prevention is worth a pound of cure. They also see that customers ultimately run their business. And no harm can come from having gay and lesbian consumers, workers, and stockholders on your company's side.

A good barometer of this axiom can be seen in the ongoing development of gay and lesbian employee groups cropping up at major corporations around the country. In the last two years, there have been six major gay and lesbian consumer and employee national workshops. At each one, new companies attended and new ideas were born in human resource and company marketing departments about real opportunities for the future.

When it comes to gay and lesbian employees and consumers, the two often go hand in hand at the corporate level.

Challenges

The disheartening news is that tens of thousands of American companies are doing business with gay and lesbian consumers and don't even know it. Many don't have gay and lesbian employee groups or even a policy statement barring discrimination against gay and lesbian employees in general. And of course, plenty of companies still exist in America where gay and lesbian employees are not out in the workplace, nor do they feel confident that their jobs would be remain secure if they did indeed come out.

With these issues left unaddressed, many companies are sitting on ticking time bombs—both in their ability to attract a talented and vibrant workforce and in their eventual capacity to compete for what will soon prove to be required marketing in all kinds of product and service industries.

Don't let your company be one that has to play catch-up with the competition when it comes to corporate common sense and sexual orientation. Gaining and keeping gay and lesbian consumers, like heterosexual consumers, is about relationship building. But in the coming years, that relationship needs to be built on much more solid ground with gay and lesbian consumers than has been traditionally necessary with heterosexual consumers.

If American companies want to attract and keep gay and lesbian consumers, then they have to learn to talk to them on a variety of commercial terrains above and beyond where the consumers are doing the majority of their spending. That begins inside the doors of the company.

As author Ed Mickens stated at the beginning of his important book, *The 100 Best Companies for Gay Men and Lesbians:*

> Employers who do well addressing gay and lesbian issues are the organizations that will excel in the years to come. They will probably outshine their competitors. They will grow and develop profitably in their industries. They will find creative new ways to flourish in the uncertain marketplace of the 1990s and likely the new millennium beyond.
> Why?
> Talent. Plus openness and an ability to change.
> This doesn't mean that companies will excel *only* because they are good with lesbian and gay issues. But it is a revealing indicator. Organizations that address gay and lesbian issues

demonstrate a willingness to listen and respond to the concerns of their employees. All their employees.[10]

Authors Sean Strub, Dan Baker, and Bill Henning also state clearly in their book, *Cracking the Corporate Closet:*

> . . . the most basic measure of how an American corporation stands on treating its lesbian and gay employees as equals is whether or not it has an anti-discrimination policy or equal employment opportunity statement that includes the term "sexual orientation" or "sexual preference."[11]

It's really that simple. Marketers interested in reaching gay and lesbian consumers must first investigate their companies' own stated policies regarding this issue. They must understand that that commitment must be communicated positively and conspicuously through a decisive and ongoing, multifaceted corporate plan of action that extends from hiring practices to the marketplace to the political landscape.

Trickle-Down Dynamics

As more gay and lesbian employee groups form at major American companies, they will eventually become involved in the marketing and planning of their respective companies in relation to gay and lesbian consumers.

Prior to the breakup of AT&T into three companies (AT&T, Lucent, and NCR) the gay and lesbian employee group at the old AT&T corporation, League (Lesbians, Bisexual, and Gay United Employees) actually co-authored with AT&T's marketing department an astonishingly shrewd 1994 direct mail appeal for long-distance service aimed directly at gay and lesbian consumers.

The appeal was mailed in a lavender envelope and used the image of a rainbow-colored phone cord on the outside with an inside headline that read, "It's time for a change." The letter came packaged with a brochure explaining AT&T's True USA Savings, True Rewards, and True Voice campaigns and was signed by AT&T's Long Distance Service Manager, Jody Gieger, and LEAGUE's two national co-chairs, Arturo Nava and Margaret Burd. It even had a postscript that read:

AT&T is pleased to be a part of Gay Games IV & Cultural
Festival, taking place in New York City this June 18-25. Come
to the Unity Center and receive a free gift.

Now that is relationship marketing. It also represents one of the best
possible examples of why the emerging gay and lesbian marketplace is really a gay and lesbian consumer revolution.

AT&T would not release sales figures for this particular campaign. However, AT&T has retained Prime Access Inc., a firm run
by Howard Buford, who was responsible for producing the groundbreaking advertising and direct mail appeal that AT&T and League
collaborated on.

According to Buford, who characterizes Prime Access Inc. as a
full-service marketing and communications company that also provides management counsel in specialized markets:

> . . . you first want to get a feel for how comfortable a client is
> with different kinds of advertising in general. Does the client
> want ambiguous advertising vs. targeted advertising in this
> market? Sometimes they surprise you.
>
> From a business perspective, what tends to drive their cor-
> porate thinking [on gay and lesbian marketplace issues] has a
> lot to do with what each manager brings to the table. Each to a
> certain degree, brings his or her own baggage to all the issues.
>
> A lot goes into the decision-making process—the manag-
> er's overall level of comfort [with gay and lesbian marketing],
> their background, their family—these things all impact on the
> overall strategy of a company.
>
> There's also the issue of the way a company traditionally
> looks at markets or interprets risk—all of which, of course,
> differs from company to company. Companies like AT&T
> want to be as appropriate as possible for as many people as
> possible.

This should be the goal of any company that wants to reach the gay
and lesbian consumer market: to be as appropriate as possible to as
many people as possible.

How to Know What Is Appropriate

An important and increasingly influential national group called GLAAD, the Gay and Lesbian Alliance Against Defamation, whose express purpose is specifically to stop defamation of gay and lesbian Americans in the media, has gained broadscale public attention and support from mainstream business. Each year the GLAAD media awards are regularly hosted and attended by celebrity talent from across the performing and media arts spectrum.

Some of GLAAD's successes over the years have included a public relations campaign mounted against Cobb County, Georgia, for an antigay and lesbian ordinance. GLAAD's efforts in conjunction with public statements made by Olympic Gold Medalist Greg Louganis resulted in the moving of scheduled 1996 Olympic events out of Cobb County. GLAAD also convinced the CBS News affiliate in San Francisco to stop using abusive and erroneous language such as "special rights" when reporting on controversial gay and lesbian discrimination ballot issues such as Colorado's Amendment 2. In addition, GLAAD was influential in helping *The New York Times* end its ban on the use of the word "gay" in its reporting. According to a recent flyer mailed to over 10,000 of GLAAD's supporters:

> Our monitoring, response, education, and visibility programs have changed the way society sees and represents gay, lesbian, and bisexual lives . . .
>
> . . . *The New York Times* wouldn't even let its reporters use the word "gay" ten years ago. Today, thanks to GLAAD the paper is an authority on the subject. So are its thousands of readers.
>
> . . . [and] Hollywood's *Basic Instinct* kept filmmakers believing that gays and lesbians had to either be invisible or in jail. GLAAD helped them find us in *Philadelphia* among other places.

In addition to preventing defamation of gays and lesbians in the media, GLAAD has also been successful in bringing together different groups within the gay and lesbian community to address a variety of issues related to the visibility of people of color.

Donald Suggs, a former director of communications for GLAAD, was very instrumental in helping to focus the organization on issues of race and gender in relation to sexual orientation. Since much of the advertising aimed at gay and lesbian Americans is often less than representative of the diversity of the entire gay and lesbian community—as is much of advertising overall—I found his remarks worth considering by marketers of all kinds.

In one meeting I had with him about race and sexual orientation, he noted:

> I don't think most black gay people see the issue of homophobia in a vacuum. For us, it's part of a larger view of how [American culture] marginalizes a lot of people. Even straight white men get old, and eventually there's a way in which older people are marginalized in this culture. If you are really committed to struggling against homophobia, then you have to be committed to struggling against all the ways in which [our culture] marginalizes people . . .
>
> I think that black gay people have a better understanding of what that dynamic is. It's not just about being able to take your lover to the company picnic. [Black people] see this whole array of ways in which this world has to be changed and transformed.
>
> [For instance], most black gay people live within the black community. Our perception of who we are is not predicated on being "out." Most black gay bars are located in the black community. Black people know those bars are there. Black people don't burn them down. I'm not saying the black community is less homophobic, I'm just saying we're homophobic in a different way. We don't define ourselves in a way that forces us to readjust or redefine what it means to be black or what your relationship to the community is. It does not take this form of "you have to leave [the community]."
>
> . . . [However], I think in a lot of white middle-class communities you do have to leave [if you're gay or lesbian]. You have to move to New York, to San Francisco, or to a different neighborhood—I think that's homophobic; it's just expressing itself differently.

Also, homosexuality is seen in a different light [for many black people]. For instance, if I meet some black men and ask if they are gay, they might say no. But if I say, are you "in the life," that's more [clear]. Saying "in the life" incorporates this whole range of behaviors, ideas, and self-perceptions that everyone encompasses [heterosexuality and homosexuality]. It is saying that you have an understanding [of many things] . . .

Donald Suggs' remarks strike a chord with many in lesbian, gay, and transgendered communities. To look at a lot of gay advertising, you would never think so. Because too much gay advertising is still white-focused, male-focused, and affluent-oriented.

But in time that will change. There was a time when companies would not advertise to many ethnic or racial groups. Today, no company in America would think of not making sure that its corporate policies are in line with the values of the majority of American citizens when it comes to issues of race, sex, and religion. Soon the same will apply to sexual orientation across the board, and it will apply to marketing, in time, as well.

It was noted earlier in this book that the Yankelovich data identifies a trend toward increasing tolerance and acceptance of gay and lesbian sexuality in the country at large. And even though Americans are generally conservative people, they are also humane and fair.

As the gay and lesbian consumer revolution makes itself more known in business through media and politics, so will more Americans come to see that the ongoing fight for equal rights for gay and lesbian Americans is simply basic to the "American experience," basic to our continually unfolding sense of a real, human-oriented heritage.

GAY AND LESBIAN CONSUMER DEMAND:
KEY AREAS OF GROWTH

As outlined from the Yankelovich research in the previous chapter, there are five general areas of significant difference that distinguish self-identifying gay and lesbian consumers from heterosexual consumers. Gay and lesbian consumers are more concerned about a focus on individuality, a need for association, and a search beyond the everyday experience; they have an extraordinary need to alleviate stress and a pronounced sense of cynicism and mistrust of institutions.

Within each of these areas (and in combination with each other) an extraordinary opportunity exists to position products and services that communicate specific benefits in relation to the differences indicated between gay consumers and straight consumers. The following are some examples of products and services that are especially well-suited for targeted marketing to gay and lesbian consumers:

- *Focus on Individuality:* All products, goods, and services that relate to the consumer's sense of identity including clothing, shoes, jewelry, cosmetics, toiletries, health care, sports and fitness, home furnishings, books, magazines, travel, psychotherapy, hobbies, crafts, home study courses, etc.
- *Need for Association:* Restaurants, theaters, clubs, group travel, health and fitness, educational and trade institutions, spiritual and religious groups, arts and crafts groups, sports clubs, dance halls, arts and entertainment events, concerts, and public fundraising drives.
- *Searching Out and Experiencing Life's Diversity:* Pay-per-view television, interactive television, computers, on-line bulletin boards and communication venues, sporting events, weekend travel, virtual reality, community events, books, magazines, new restaurants, clubs and entertainment opportunities, theater, opera, music, dance, and performance art.
- *Stress Alleviation:* Sundries, music, gourmet food and cooking supplies, sporting events, clothing and accessories, home sporting equipment, jogging shoes, massage therapy, acupuncture, aromatherapy, arts and crafts, aerobics, gymnastics, swimming, hiking and camping gear, and clothing.
- *Skepticism and Mistrust:* Products that promote understanding and alleviate stress, home security systems, pets and pet care supplies, self-defense courses, financial services, and investment opportunities.

These are just a few of the products that stand to sell well to gay and lesbian consumers if marketed in a fashion that communicates or relates to the areas of difference described. In general, however, there are certain issues to bear in mind when developing campaigns for products and services aimed at this population based on these research findings.

GENERAL STRATEGY

Focusing on how great your company is in relation to gay and lesbian employment issues is never in a company's best interest. It is expected that your company is decent if you already advertise to gay and lesbian consumers. When it comes to tooting a company's own horn in these areas, the understated "addendum approach" is best.

For instance, reserve your postscript in the direct marketing letter to remind the gay or lesbian consumer that your company has domestic partnership benefits, or supports a particular organization. But playing up the issue makes it sound as if you've done a favor for the consumer. Perhaps you have. But consumers want to give you their money for your good products and services, not congratulations for your good moral deeds in the marketplace.

Focus first and foremost on your product or service and its benefits to the gay and lesbian consumer. Give concrete examples of what you mean by quality. State how your product makes life easier, more enjoyable, fashionable, beautiful, comforting, etc. Explain the details that distinguish your product or service from your competition. Don't be afraid to use humor.

Some industries such as fashion, food and beverage, and even home furnishings are able to pull off the use of aesthetic extremes such as zany camera angles, wild lighting, female impersonation, etc. Conservative companies of course will focus more seriously on product appeal, stature, and dependability.

But it must be remembered that gay and lesbian consumers are fast studies, quick to see through hollow appeals and misguided marketing. If a company has done its homework, has consulted with competent marketing counsel, and has encouraged the input of gay and lesbian employees or even customers, it will all shine through in the advertising and the sales.

Advertising and Direct Marketing Copy

As with most advertising copy, keeping it as short as possible is the general order of the times. With gay and lesbian consumers, even shorter is better.

As a rule, gay and lesbian consumers are very discerning individuals. They get the point fast. So don't spend endless time getting to the point—unless the product or service genuinely demands a longer story line. If you must incorporate a lot of copy into a print display advertisement or a direct mail campaign, use bold titles followed by short bullet points to break up the copy.

Advertising Imagery

Keep the use of canned gay and lesbian imagery to a minimum. Much of the commonly seen advertising aimed at gay and lesbian consumers today such as pink triangles, rainbow flags, and the color lavender have definitely been a trend for the past eight years, although they are largely the domain of gay- and lesbian-owned companies. This imagery means different things to different people.

The use of inverted pink triangles (which the Nazis used in concentration camps to identify homosexuals) is risky. I would particularly advise against the use of pink triangles by any major corporation unless that corporation's history with gay and lesbian consumers is stellar. Few companies are really in a strong enough moral or political position to sprinkle pink triangles around like computer clip art.

The risk of sending the wrong message is simply too great. Many older gay and lesbian Americans, particularly veterans, may be offended by their use on behalf of big business.

Sending the Correct Message

Products and services advertised to gay and lesbian consumers must ultimately say two things:

1. Our product is right for you because it offers more value for the dollar.
2. Our company is right for you because we have integrity on matters of sexual orientation.

Marketers must also remember that in the back of every gay and lesbian consumer's mind is (in varying degrees) the accurate perception that mainstream society has historically not been tolerant of his or her individuality. Also a potential sea of mixed feelings exists in the consumer's mind about sexual expression, social tolerance for sexual expression, its relationship to AIDS, and the public's perception of AIDS in relation to homosexuality. When a gay or lesbian consumer is confronted with marketing imagery and advertising messages from your company, any background perceptions of intolerance must be minimized in relation to the company name or product branding.

These are politically charged times for gay and lesbian Americans. Each individual gay or lesbian person's experience, degree of outness, financial independence, etc., all affect the perception of the brand and the willingness to respond to its positioning. These issues have changed in the minds of gay and lesbian consumers over the past two decades, but especially so during the past ten years.

Prior to Randy Shilts's *And the Band Played On,* the best-selling gay-themed books were *The Joy of Gay Sex* and Jonathan Katz's *Gay American History* which sold, according to St. Martins editor Michael Denenny "something like 80 to 90 thousand copies." Denenny says that those figures "used to be my benchmark. If you had a best-seller in the gay and lesbian market you would get up around [that number of copies]."

What is particularly telling for marketers is what has occurred between the days of the best-selling *The Joy of Gay Sex* and the equally best-selling *And the Band Played On*—about sixteen years. Within that time, hundreds of thousands of gay and lesbian Americans came out of the closet and celebrated in the gay and lesbian liberation movement in modern America. In many ways *The Joy of Gay Sex* symbolically represented in marketing numbers the celebration of that social unfolding.

The numbers are equally telling in the way the story has ended for so many. This fact has remained in the gay and lesbian consumer's mind. In that short sixteen years, the enormity of the AIDS crisis and the horror of its devastation are literally bookended in sales figures that speak for themselves and cast a broad-ranging commentary on gay and lesbian culture. Two of the best-selling books in gay and lesbian America practically chronicle the birth of gay liberation and, since then, the deaths of more than all who died in Vietnam.

The theme of gay and lesbian visibility and its relationship to the AIDS crisis in America ran strong, like a steel cable, through nearly every interview I conducted for this book. It was particularly apparent in my discussion with editor Michael Denenny, who edited Randy Shilts's giant success *And the Band Played On* as well as countless other successful gay and lesbian (and nongay) titles. In conversations about *And the Band Played On*, Randy Shilts, AIDS, and all that has happened in American gay and lesbian culture, one particular moment will stay with me forever. It was when Denenny remarked slowly, while staring across my shoulder into what felt like a realm miles away from his manuscript-flooded office:

> I can remember in 1967 when three gay men could not congregate on a street corner. Stonewall was only twenty-five years ago, and I've only been publishing gay books for sixteen years. The difference in the sixteen years is enormous.
>
> I'm concerned about the consolidation of the gay audience, the gay imagination, the consolidation of the gay spiritual life for want of a better term . . .

Companies targeting gay consumers need to ask themselves important questions in relationship to what the "consolidation of the gay and lesbian audience" means to them.

To target gay and lesbian Americans as consumers is to target America's youth, American war veterans, parents, brothers and sisters, people of color, Jews, Christians, Hispanics, those with disabilities, and people living with HIV, AIDS, or breast cancer. To target gay and lesbian Americans is to conduct business with many different kinds of people—many of whom are perpetually grieving the loss of an entire generation of their friends and loved ones to AIDS.

Gay and lesbian consumers notice what is marketed to them. That is by no means to say that every advertising message has to be socially and politically correct; but it does have to be "emotionally informed" with a sense of realism about modern gay and lesbian culture.

This brings us to the development and portrayal of accurate images and characterizations of gay and lesbian consumers in marketing and advertising communications.

Be Real; Be Matter-of-Fact

Michael Kaminer, of Michael Kaminer Public Relations, a firm with a solid track record in handling publicity for gay and straight clients, remarked to me once about how to handle gay and lesbian clients:

> Well, I have approached and handled my gay and lesbian accounts the way I handle my other accounts. It all requires micromanagement, but at the same time I cast as wide a net as possible. I never assume anybody is homophobic; I never assume anybody will hang up on me. But I do look out for coded advertising, because I hate it. If companies are going after this market, they can't insult; they can't use euphemism. Gay consumers have some of the strongest bullshit detectors around.

Indeed, consider an innocently placed advertisement for a restaurant in a local gay and lesbian news publication showing two muscle-studded white boys in tank tops spoon-feeding each other strawberries dripping with whipped cream. It may appear attractive to some gay men, even cute to some straight people in general. But if it does not run concurrently every other week showing women and people of color in the same scenario, it is probably driving a certain clientele away from the establishment (which was located in a very integrated New York City neighborhood).

I recently saw an advertisement on the side of a truck in New York that showed a handsome man dancing with a beautiful woman. The man was wearing a tuxedo and the woman was wearing a long flowing gown. They had smiles on their faces. It was truly a lovely picture. Then I noticed the headline, which said "Man At His Best."

The implication was subtle, but indicative of why gay and lesbian consumers are cynical about advertising, media imagery, and mainstream culture in general. The advertisement could have been made all the more shrewd and potentially less insulting if it simply had said, "A Man At His Best," meaning the singular man in the picture, a single example of a man at his personal best—not all men.

This is the kind of mistake that marketers cannot afford to make when targeting gay and lesbian consumers. No doubt, equal opportunity advertising does not have to be the rule when it comes to marketing. Not all products and services are intended for everyone. Not all products and services can be successfully marketed to gay and lesbian consumers. The key is to strike a happy medium between the representation of, or the "communication of a corporate understanding of" social and sexual diversity in marketing imagery and the product or service benefits.

Details magazine is particularly adept at striking this sensitive balance in both its imagery and its editorial copy. Its editors have a solid understanding of who their market is: men—gay and straight (and some women)—and they direct their energies toward casting a wide enough net not to offend anyone yet focus on enough specifics to attract a broad range of men and women. This philosophy is even in their name.

According to an editor at *Details*, "Sensitivity is an issue. We wouldn't do something if it's going to offend a certain segment of the population—any segment of the population. At *Details*, there's a '*Details* guy' that everyone sort of has in the back of his mind. And I think [as a concept] that he can be pretty bisexual . . . "

It's no secret that young gay men like *Details* magazine. Yet *Details* is not known as a gay man's magazine; nor is it known as a magazine for "good ol' boys." It is a magazine for all men.

Striking a balance is not always easy to do. But it is essential.

According to Jeanne Cordova, publisher of the Los Angeles Gay and Lesbian Community Yellow Pages, which contains every kind of advertising imaginable and fills an important and unique niche in

Southern California, "What major companies need to do to is [become more informed about] lesbian sensibility. [They need to show] two women together or single women dressed the way a lesbian [might] dress."

Cordova, who had her own publication in the 1970s called *Lesbian Tide,* also agrees that there is a connection between being aligned with the gay and lesbian community and conducting business with gay and lesbian consumers. She commented about women's issues in particular, "Companies need to be willing to make contributions specifically to lesbian groups."

This is one of the most important issues that marketers often leave unaddressed. There are in fact more women in the world than men. And even if you are only targeting gay men—you are also targeting a large HIV population and a certain number of black and Hispanic gay men as well.

HIV AND THE GAY MARKETING MOMENT

Jay Blotcher, an activist and New York writer, characterizes the issue of AIDS in an interesting way. He sees a relationship between marketing and the gay and lesbian fight for visibility, equal rights, and an end to the AIDS crisis, commenting:

> . . . you have to go back to the connection between AIDS and this market. You'd be hard pressed to say what AIDS did that was good for the community, but it did spark this amazing awareness, awareness that forced people out of the closet and forced a mainstream consciousness of gays and lesbians. It brought people out.
>
> If you look at old copies of *After Dark* in the mid-seventies, marketing to gay people was happening in a big way, and I would contend that AIDS is what dropped the big black curtain on it all in the early 80s. Because in the 1970s mainstream fashion and films, colognes, etc., were putting money into this community.
>
> It was already happening long before AIDS.

Blotcher is absolutely right. All through the 1970s, *After Dark,* a national entertainment magazine with an overwhelming gay and lesbian readership (a kind of loose—what would have been politically incorrect—version of *OUT* magazine, for the bell-bottom years) enjoyed major attention from all kinds of high-profile advertisers.

After Dark enjoyed advertisers reflective of that era: Metro-Goldwyn-Mayer Inc.; the RCA Records division of RCA Corporation; Paramount Pictures Corporation, a (then) subsidiary of Gulf & Western Industries Inc.; Columbia Pictures; Twentieth-Century-Fox Film Corporation; Warner Brothers, Carnegie Hall, and the New York City Ballet.

Liquor was being advertised in the pages of *The Advocate*, the Hearst Corporation had begun printing paperbacks of interest to gay and lesbian consumers through their Avon Books division, and Bantam was offering seven different books as well—one of which was *The Front Runner* by Patricia Warren. The rights to the film had been purchased by Paul Newman. In fact, at the time, book publishers were printing at least ten times as many gay and lesbian-themed books as at the time of the Stonewall Riots just six years earlier.[12] In New York City new luxury high-rise residences were openly marketing their exclusive real estate to gay and lesbian consumers. As early as 1975, *The Wall Street Journal* reported on these developments in an article titled "Campaigns to Sell to Homosexual Market Are Being Launched by More Big Firms."[13] The *Journal* wrote:

> . . . this might have been hard to imagine only a few years ago. But today, American business is starting once-unthinkable projects—campaigns to reach the homosexual market. The trend is spotty, but dozens of major companies are taking steps.

As an interesting commentary on how times have changed, the same article quoted a Bloomingdale's spokesperson on what was then a fashionable new product the retailer had begun offering, the licensing of bath towels for the (then popular and still in business) Continental Baths of New York City. The article quoted a store representative as saying: "This is one of the campiest things we have ever done. . . ."

But those days are over. Much pain is still running through America's gay and lesbian community.

Marketers need to stay mindful that they are dealing with sensitive issues when they go about promoting products and services to gay consumers. But they also do not need to handle gay and lesbian consumers with kid gloves. There is no need to walk on eggshells with marketing messaging. It is important to be out with the message. Not conflicted, coded, or in any way closeted about the fact that you are targeting them.

The explosion of gay and lesbian marketing goes hand in hand with the surge in gay and lesbian activism in the past five years.

As Blotcher also noted:

> [This marketing trend] started up again in the late 80s.
>
> There's so many things that [happened]. Gay people were turning into a political force and a culture force after Stonewall. It was about the clubs and the clothes. About 1989/1990 suddenly it was our world again. Andy Rooney stuff, the rappers doing antigay stuff, marketing started again, but you saw people denying what they were doing, the advertising was [subtle].
>
> It was all beginning to resurge with AIDS activism, queer nation, and the films that were coming out. . . .
>
> But then again, with the awareness, gays and lesbians weren't happy with [films such as] *Basic Instinct* and they were unhappy about *The Silence of the Lambs* . . .
>
> . . . and then the boycotts, its disputable what impact the boycotts have had specifically, but the awareness [of these companies' positions] was coming out.
>
> And as always, change does not start just with gays, it starts with the arts. So we were very shrewd in ACT UP, but also with Queer Nation, we knew that the arts eventually affect everything else and so [focused some of our activist work there].
>
> More changes of heart come with a good film than a law being passed. [Some believe] *Philadelphia* did more for activism and AIDS than all the demonstrations up until then, [which was the motivation behind going] after the arts.
>
> [Then] people broke into Burroughs Wellcome, and bolted themselves into a room, handcuffed themselves, saying they were going to have a standoff and stay in there until "you

lower the price of AZT," and within an hour they were dragged out by the police . . . that was the beginning.

Then there were [more] demos and then came the demo at the stock exchange, all that stuff. Not letting up the pressure finally sparked the media, including *The New York Times* editorial on [the] greediness and profit mongering [of Burroughs Wellcome], and when *The New York Times* is creating nicks in your shining reputation, that's when things change. That's when Burroughs Wellcome cried "uncle" and lowered the price [of AZT].

[Anyway, activist] news is one thing—gay stuff creeping into mainstream sitcoms is the legacy of activism. We're making gay issues a big deal now, so one day they won't have to be.

Chapter 6

Key Cities and Emerging
Opportunities for Business

*A company that puts back into the community is going to
win no matter what.*

Francis Stevens, Editor—*Curve*

To target gay and lesbian consumers is to target America's cities—both large and small. The greatest portion of self-identifying
gay and lesbian Americans live in the cities. And like heterosexual
Americans, they spend, on average, the greatest portion of their
total income on rental housing or homeowner mortgages.

Nationally oriented real estate brokerage firms in the United States
have not yet made a serious effort to market to gays and lesbians as a
target group through gay and lesbian media. Yet real estate and rental
property plays an important role in the maintenance and growth of
gay and lesbian neighborhoods across America.

In addition, the majority of America's local gay and lesbian newspapers are located in the highest property value areas of the country,
yet generally charge the least expensive rates per column inch of
advertising space for those areas.

Independent real estate agents report that the presence of gays and
lesbians in certain areas of the United States actually increases property values. They further report that gays and lesbians often help to
reestablish small neighborhood economies—many of which later
become important major areas of business commerce and long-term
urban and cultural renewal.

The explosion of neighborhood revitalization in relation to gay
and lesbian consumerism in cities across the United States has been

documented by many major newspapers. Strong gay and lesbian neighborhoods also attract business and conventions to cities that might not otherwise enjoy such a large influx of revenue if not for this phenomenon.

A recent article in *The New York Times*[1] titled "Gay Presence Leads Revival of Declining Neighborhoods" read in part:

> . . . predominantly gay neighborhoods have arisen in a dozen major cities over the last two decades, at once bolstering those cities' sagging tax bases, pumping thousands of dollars into the economy and sometimes making tired neighborhoods safer and more attractive to heterosexuals.

This rise in stature in neighborhoods across America has had an immeasurable effect on the growth and stability of pivotal inner-city neighborhoods. There is, however, somewhat of a downside. With the rise of visibility in these areas—many of which include homes from the turn of the last century valued in the millions of dollars—there has been the added perpetuation of the stereotype that gays and lesbians are more affluent than they really are. This local visibility of gay and lesbian Americans living in affluent or "fashionable" neighborhoods combines with the distorted rhetoric of right-wing radicals and misrepresented gay newspaper statistics, leaving the impression that gay and lesbian Americans have more money than they actually do. Although it is true that tens of thousands of gays and lesbians are homeowners in the United States, so are heterosexuals—hundreds of thousands, plenty of whom live in the cities as well.

Still, that challenge aside, as a group, gays and lesbians tend to move to larger urban areas where property values eventually become higher. This trend was especially noticeable, in varying degrees, from 1972 to 1995 in the following areas:

- Montrose and Heights neighborhoods in Houston
- Oaklawn in Dallas
- Cheesman Park area in Denver
- Seattle's Capitol Hill area
- Liberty Hill in Cincinnati

- The Grand Street area in St. Louis
- Greenwich Village, Soho, Brooklyn Heights, and Park Slope in New York City
- Hollywood, West Hollywood, Silverlake, and Venice Beach in Los Angeles
- In and around the Old Town and Lincoln Park areas of Chicago
- Lockerbie Square and the Near North Side of Indianapolis
- Ft. Lauderdale, Florida and South Beach in Miami
- Dupont Circle in Washington, DC
- Northern Liberties area and Graduate Hospital/South of South Street in Philadelphia
- Numerous neighborhoods in San Francisco, CA
- The French Quarter in New Orleans

Of the entire self-identified gay and lesbian population in the United States, more are likely to be homeowners in larger urban areas because such areas are simply more known for being—or are within driving distance of—widely recognized gay and lesbian centers of culture.

The neighborhoods listed above will continue to be important gay and lesbian population growth regions into the next century, however. The following list of cities overall can also be expected to experience a fast and profound level of gay and lesbian population growth—equally emerging (some rapidly) as important nationally recognized centers of lesbian and gay male cultural and economic renewal throughout the next century: Baltimore, Maryland; Miami, Ft. Lauderdale, Jacksonville, Tampa, and St. Petersburg in Florida; Atlanta and Savannah, Georgia; Corpus Christi, Austin, El Paso, Ft. Worth, and San Antonio in Texas; Sacramento, San Diego, San Jose, Monterey, Long Beach, and Palm Springs in California; New Orleans; Minneapolis/St. Paul, Minnesota; Columbus, Ohio; Portland, Oregon; Nashville and Memphis in Tennessee; Albuquerque, New Mexico; Madison and Milwaukee in Wisconsin; Philadelphia, Pittsburgh, and New Hope, Pennsylvania; Boston and Provincetown, Massachusetts; Little Rock, Arkansas; Providence, Rhode Island; Bloomington, Indiana; Detroit, Michigan; Greenwich, Connecticut; all areas on Long Island, New York, all areas of New Jersey from Hoboken to the shore;

Charlotte, North Carolina; Honolulu; Oklahoma City, Oklahoma; and Kansas City, Missouri.

Each of these areas of the United States is experiencing, in varying degrees, new surges of gay and lesbian cultural visibility—most also have a lower cost of living as well—making them attractive cities for gay and lesbian Americans to reside in as an alternative to the larger gay and lesbian "mecca cities."

INVESTING IN TASTE

Gay and lesbian Americans spend the second largest portion of their total income on food and beverages—whether purchased in restaurants and clubs or as groceries from local supermarkets.

Alcoholic beverages, restaurants, and clubs—combined with other small businesses—make up the largest proportion of display advertising in numerous gay and lesbian publications across the country.

Although there is no reason to believe that gays and lesbians would not widely clip savings coupons for groceries from local gay and lesbian news publications, relatively few grocery chains take advantage of the opportunities local gay and lesbian newspapers offer.

Although some scattered local supermarkets have advertised in gay and lesbian newspapers, no major food chain to date has launched a broadscale gay and lesbian advertising campaign. This area marks one of the most untapped market niches in the entire food and beverage industry—especially in light of Yankelovich data showing gay and lesbian interest in gourmet cooking, home entertaining, and the home in general as a place of security and community socializing.

Local restaurants however, especially those owned and operated in predominantly gay and lesbian neighborhoods, have enjoyed monumental success advertising their businesses in local gay and lesbian newspapers.

The average startup cost for a midsized restaurant in the United States is around $200,000. Weekly revenue in a busy restaurant can even out around thirty to forty thousand in well-populated locations.

With the average quarter-page advertisement in most gay and lesbian newsweekly publications running less than $250, newly opened restaurants would be smart to make advertising to the gay and lesbian market a major priority. In many gay and lesbian neighborhoods, and in neighborhoods adjacent to gay and lesbian population centers, a new restaurant's success or failure often hinges on their understanding of and marketing to gay and lesbian consumers.

This is not necessarily because gay and lesbian consumers are more likely to eat out. It is because they represent the largest cross section of the entire population for a given geographic area (African Americans and other minorities, Generation X, Baby Boomers, seniors, families, businesspeople, etc.).

The trend lately toward segmentation of advertising spending in the promotion of bottled water through sponsorship of gay and lesbian events and advertising in gay and lesbian publications is driven in part by the degree to which this market segment offers a wide range of marketplace visibility. In 1987, Naya bottled water from Nora Beverage Company was the first bottled water to be openly targeted to gays and lesbians in the United States. A regional campaign was promoted through the gay and lesbian press and since that time Nora Beverage has promoted Naya at gay and lesbian pride celebrations each year.

According to a Nora Beverage representative, "We try and keep away from politics or direct social commentary on groups in general, but [we certainly] support basic human rights."

Indeed they do. Naya maintained and even heightened its visibility within the gay and lesbian community when it launched a shrewd relationship marketing effort at a critical time: they provided complimentary water at the March on Washington in April 1993.

Evidently the other water bottlers are beginning to wise up. By 1994 Nora Beverage began to see the pronounced emergence of bottled water competition across the United States—including Evian, Perrier, and Calistoga.

Drivers on sales routes across the country still report increasing sales of Naya water in known gay and lesbian neighborhoods such as those listed above. It is clear that gays and lesbians know who supported them first and are continuing to purchase Naya out of loyalty.

Since food and beverage industries are the second largest area of gay and lesbian spending in the United States, other food and beverage producers, restaurants, grocery stores, and neighborhood convenience marts should consider aiming their products at gays and lesbians, particularly through gay and lesbian regional newspapers, while brand loyalty establishment time is still available. Quarterly and annually printed regional gay and lesbian advertiser guides, yellow pages, and neighborhood directories also provide excellent ways to reach these consumers across the country.

According to Robb Davis, president and publisher of the highly successful Metrosource, a comprehensive magazine-like community resource of businesses in the New York City metropolitan area, "the people that advertise in Metrosource tell us they get results. [Our] ideal advertiser is service oriented.

"I know you've heard this before, but there is a segment of the population that really wants to support the people that advertise in [local] gay and lesbian publications. There are a lot of [gay and lesbian consumers] out there who feel that if a company is genuinely being supportive, that their products and services should be [bought first]. Obviously it's in my interest to believe that, but I think that because of people's pride in the community they want to support [all kinds of] products that are being aimed at them."

Absolut Vodka certainly learned that lesson long ago as one of the first leading alcoholic beverage products to be marketed to gay and lesbian consumers. Michel Roux, president and chief executive officer of Carillon Importers, Ltd., was one of the pioneering advertisers that helped bring heightened brand visibility and a dependable source of revenue to gay and lesbian publications in the United States. It was through Michel Roux's import company that Absolut, Gran Marnier, and Bombay Gin first made their appearances in *The Advocate* in the late 1970s.

Although Absolut is still the number one purchased vodka today among gay and lesbian Americans (and other consumers as well), Carillon lost its distribution rights to Absolut when Vin and Spirit, the Swedish state-owned producer, abruptly moved the Absolut brand to Seagram.

After that, Roux moved to acquire the distribution rights to Stolichnaya Vodka, which was actually the leading vodka prior to Roux's miracle work with Absolut. Roux, in association with advertising agency Margeotes, Fertitta, Donaher, and Weiss, has produced a compelling campaign for Stolichnaya that is also using the gay and lesbian marketplace to compete against Absolut.

Roux's marketing philosophy has not changed. "In time, people will realize we are there and that we are supporting the gay community. It takes a further commitment. A marketer should also be supporting the gay community in areas such as civil rights, AIDS research, and political equality." Under Roux's stewardship, the Stoli brand has associated itself with DIFFA (Design Industry's Foundation for AIDS), God's Love We Deliver, and the North American Gay Volleyball Association Championship Tournament.

Other leading alcoholic beverages include Miller, Budweiser, Rolling Rock, Amstel Light, Remy Martin, Hennessy Cognac, Dewars White Label Scotch, Godiva Liqueur, and Campari. There are many others.

Gays and lesbians are shown in some survey data to participate in a higher consumption of tobacco-related products, although tobacco companies have traditionally shied away from buying advertising in gay and lesbian publications. In 1994 Parliament and Benson and Hedges advertising began to appear in *OUT* magazine. Marlboro and Winston outdoor advertising is also relatively conspicuous in gay and lesbian neighborhoods around the country.

HEALTHY LIVING

Entire books have been written on gay and lesbian health care, AIDS, and the relationships between the politics of big business marketing and the bureaucracy of government involvement (or lack of involvement).

The state of health care in the gay and lesbian community exists, by design, at a distinct disadvantage in comparison to the health care enjoyed by heterosexuals—mainly to the extent that most gays and lesbians cannot share employment-related health care benefits with their lovers or companions in the same way the heterosexuals can with their legally recognized spouses through most American companies' benefits packages.

As indicated previously, in some companies this is changing. Domestic partnership benefits in the workplace allow unmarried partners to sign up for benefits through group health insurance programs in the same way that heterosexual married partners do.

According to Richard Mayora, an account executive at HBO and a coordinator with Lesbians and Gay Men (the gay and lesbian employee group at Time Warner), domestic partnership benefits became available at HBO in July 1993. "It was the chairman's decision [to do this]. He thought it was the equitable thing to do."

At that time, Time Warner owned forty-four different companies including Time Inc., Time Magazines, Home Box Office, Warner Music Group, Warner Pictures, Time-Warner Cable, Atlantic Records, Elektra, and Sire records—not all which have domestic partnership benefits, for a variety of organizational and financial reasons too lengthy to discuss here.

Mayora characterizes the environment: "You're talking about forty-four different companies at Time Warner—in many cases, very different from each other, with differing corporate climates. [However], at HBO specifically, management has been top-notch in every way in terms of policies, [particularly] AIDS, and very understanding when it comes to benefits [in general]."

Considering the monumental amount of work, frustration, and rage that activists, health care professionals, caregivers, and families and friends have felt, AIDS as a marketplace issue cannot possibly be discussed or even remotely characterized in a preliminary fashion within the context of this book without insulting the experiences, challenges, hardships, and grief being experienced by the gay and lesbian community in general.

AIDS has hit the gay and lesbian community hard as a populational cohort, as it has the African-American and Hispanic American communities as well. The crisis obviously is taking a toll on a number of socioeconomic levels, and raises enormous questions about the state of health care in the United States overall.

Because health care within the gay and lesbian community cannot be looked at without including the marketplace issues related to AIDS, it would be hard to place a dollar volume or emphasis on key areas of growth. But clearly there are industries targeting gay and lesbian consumers—most visibly, major insurance and health care providers, private practice physicians and specialized medical professionals, viatical service insurance brokers, pharmaceuticals, health and fitness foods, vitamins, and private psychotherapy counseling.

The 1970s and 1980s saw a pronounced increase in the number of psychotherapists offering their services exclusively to gay and lesbian consumers. And in light of the 1993 Yankelovich MONITOR Gay and Lesbian Perspective analysis of the psychology of disenfranchisement, it would not seem far-fetched that gays and lesbians are spending disproportionate dollars on maintaining their mental and physical health. Every major gay and lesbian community in the United States can claim several heath and fitness gyms or exercise facilities that cater predominantly to gay and lesbian health and sports enthusiasts.

The Los Angeles metropolitan area alone has at least ten different gyms and sports facilities with an almost exclusively gay or lesbian clientele. Some are gay-owned, promoted, and operated. The same can be said for New York City, Chicago, San Francisco, and Miami. This of course presents unique opportunities for sportswear and sports equipment manufacturers, and producers of health-related food and beverage products.

ENTERTAINING THE MASSES

Because gay and lesbian Americans have a strong need to connect within their community, entertainment—not surprisingly—is a principal area of focus that is fueling marketplace activity in areas that are literally too many to mention. The most obvious and consistent area of entertainment by far, dating back to the nineteenth century, is the phenomenon of the gay bar.

Although less of a social focus in large cities than in previous years, gay and lesbian nightclubs, restaurants, dance halls, and bars still constitute a major focus of economic activity in midsized and smaller cities across the United States.

In smaller communities where there are no gay and lesbian community centers, the gay bar is still an especially important social institution, and, of course, a principal area of interest for cigarette, beer, and liquor distributors as well as the restaurants, gift shops, hardware stores, pet supply stores, and pharmacies that cater to gay and lesbian consumers in those neighborhoods.

But as shown by the astounding success of numerous Broadway plays and major box office hits in the movie industry in the past five years, gay and lesbian culture is moving beyond the local bar and more toward the mainstream of life. This trend is much more noticeable in larger cities, but even the constant introduction of new gay and lesbian characters in prime-time television indicates that this is changing.

WHAT TO WEAR

The 1990s finally saw the emergence of fashion advertising aimed directly at gay and lesbian consumers through print media purchased in gay and lesbian publications. Part of this trend is related to a relaxation of some of the fashion industry's leading designers' homophobic attitudes toward gay and lesbian newspaper and magazine publishing, which has long been supported almost exclusively by sexually oriented phone sex advertising.

As the sexually oriented advertising has begun to disappear from the pages of national gay and lesbian publications, the fashion advertising appears to have likewise increased. Not only has sexually oriented advertising all but vanished from national gay magazines, but the writing and design quality and distribution of the national glossies has improved as well. For instance, at *OUT* magazine, most of the designers, writers, advertising managers, and distribution consultants had strong backgrounds in the mainstream magazine industry prior to joining the publication—which is obvious in the book's overall look and performance.

OUT magazine has done the most by far to set the modern tone and put the wheels in motion to attract and keep new advertisers— particularly fashion advertisers—appearing in its pages.

Harry Taylor, former advertising director for *OUT* magazine, has had a historical influence in this particular area. Beginning his career in retail trade publishing with *Discount Store News*, the bible of mass market retailing, Taylor eventually emerged as a force at *Spin* magazine, the rock and roll glossy, where he worked mainly in fashion and fragrance categories. At *OUT* he started as co-advertising director.

According to Taylor, one the reasons that *OUT* has been successful is that a large portion of the staff came from other large, mainstream publications where the professional environment, aesthetic standards, and marketplace competition were much tougher than the environments traditionally found at many gay and lesbian publishing firms.

Harry Taylor says that in the earlier years, "The gay and lesbian magazine industry suffered in the eyes of advertisers as looking 'the way that gay media looked'—less than professional, production quality not up to par, inundated with sexually oriented advertising, editorial quality below that of mainstream media.

"[Those publications were] basically compiled by well-intended [people] who were doing the best service for the [gay and lesbian community] that they possibly could based on the funds they were being paid."

According to Taylor, *OUT* changed all that, saying "Right now they are not up against anything that is any more difficult than any other magazine in America. Some accounts return phone calls and others don't. It's now no different here than it is at *Details, Spin, Rolling Stone,* or somewhere else.

"[Gay people] have obviously made inroads, we are in corporate America and corporate America is supporting our markets. Homophobia is still there, but more so in the beginning than now.

"Today we get excuses like, your circulation is too small. Some advertisers tried to cover up their homophobia in the beginning. But today companies tell us point blank if advertising is an issue of homophobia [with the client]. We've developed really good relationships with advertising [agencies] who now have a level of trust with our advertising sales force. They know we aren't going to go out [and] suggest boycotts of corporations [just because they're not ready to advertise yet]."

Today a number of popular manufacturers and fashion designers of men's and women's clothing are actively courting the gay and lesbian consumer market—either through the pages of *OUT* and other gay and lesbian publications, or through mainstream fashion and lifestyle publications, outdoor advertising, and direct mail efforts.

However, besides those advertising in *OUT*, few clothing companies are candid about how they are actually targeting gay and lesbian consumers in the mainstream. Many gay and lesbian consumers feel the tug of coded advertising they believe is often aimed at them—but in an insulting, closeted way.

Interestingly, few major fashion houses in New York City would return numerous phone calls regarding their marketing philosophy for discussion in this book. In fact, a number of top designers, especially those very popular within the gay and lesbian community, refused to grant permission to reprint their ads in this book. Representatives of top designers either refused to discuss the fashion business in relationship to the gay and lesbian consumer, did not return phone calls and faxes, or outright declined to discuss the nature of their advertising philosophy altogether.

Fashion is one of the single most visible industries in the mainstream marketplace—often responsible for some of the most pronounced gay- or lesbian-sensitive imagery in American media. It is rife with suggestions of homoeroticism, androgyny, and same-sex romantic titillation. And gays and lesbians spend millions of dollars on clothing from these designers each year.

Yet it wasn't until the mid-1990s that much of Seventh Avenue genuinely began acknowledging its gay and lesbian customers and employees. Indeed for the longest time it seemed some designers were more obsessed with closets than the clothing they design to put in them. One particular company, once famous for pushing drab cotton durables in a fussy faux-jungle atmosphere, actually produced a series of ads showing same-sex couples holding each other in forlorn romantic poses.

The campaign was not bad. It garnered a lot of attention and support from gay and lesbian consumers. But then suddenly it disappeared. At the time, that company caustically declined to confirm or deny that any of its marketing approaches ever had anything to do with gays or lesbians specifically. I'm told they received phone calls from more than a few disgruntled journalists and employees about their workplace policies. At last check, the company had quietly installed domestic partner health care coverage.

GAY AND LESBIAN TRAVEL

Gays and lesbians travel a lot, both domestically and overseas. This fact presents enormous opportunities for marketers—especially in areas known for gay and lesbian vacation travel within the United States, such as Los Angeles, San Francisco, New York City, Provincetown, Massachusetts, Key West and Miami, Florida, New Orleans, Seattle, Hawaii, the U.S. Virgin Islands, Atlanta, and Washington, DC.

There are literally hundreds of gay- and lesbian-owned travel agents operating in the United States with some 330 registered specifically with the IGTA (International Gay Travel Association). In one survey of 330 travel agent members, of which 104 responded (seventy-seven owners or independent contractors, twenty-seven employees), $324,389,000 worth of business per year was reported, or an average of $3,119,125 each.

According to the IGTA, extrapolating this out to the 330 travel agents who were members of IGTA at that time creates a total agent revenue per year of over a billion dollars—$1,029,311,250 (and that is not counting travel agents used by gays and lesbians who are not currently IGTA members).

The travel industry by far is one of the leading progressive industries affecting gay and lesbian economics, policies, and business marketing decisions in important companies in the United States.

Things are looking good and changing rapidly, according to John D'alessandro, president of Out & Travel—a specialist in the domestic and international gay and lesbian travel market who has advised American Airlines and Northwest Airlines. "I would have to make this point—there are two airlines that come to mind very quickly as very pro [gay and lesbian]. I have to say first and foremost that Virgin Atlantic is a major player within this market even though many don't see them as a major domestic player, and in the U.S. [perhaps] they're not. And of course—are you sitting down? American Airlines.

"American Airlines provides a very interesting scenario. I hate even mentioning it, but American Airlines in many ways took a very serious look at the gay and lesbian marketplace because of negative incidents that happened."

There were in fact three negative incidents during the past few years. One involved the alleged firing of an employee based on sexual orientation. The second surrounded the nationally reported debacle over the forced removal of an American Airlines passenger living with AIDS. The third, and perhaps most pivotal, was the changing of linens on an aircraft that had completed its scheduled flight to Washington, DC, during the 1993 gay and lesbian equal rights march.

According to D'alessandro, "The fact of the matter [is], that each of the [incidents] caused scenes that no American carrier [wants to have to deal with]. But in the case of American Airlines, they were very very quickly [and appropriately] dealt with."

As D'alessandro characterized it, "One flight attendant out of 100,000 made a bad call, a silly bad call—which got leaked to the press—which is very interesting, but within forty-eight hours Mr. Crandall himself sent a letter to all employees."

This letter was one of the most responsibly administered corporate public relations moves on behalf of any American company and stands as an example of how companies should respond to such challenges.

On April 29, 1993, Crandall wrote:

> . . . We have an aggressive policy of nondiscrimination against any individual or group of individuals, and this policy explicitly forbids discrimination for reasons of sexual preference. This policy is especially appropriate for American because we have one of the most diverse work groups in America.
>
> . . . American Airlines apologizes to anyone who was offended by the unfortunate actions of the few employees involved in this unhappy incident. Their actions do not reflect American Airlines' policy or practice, and everyone has my pledge that we will do everything possible to ensure such lapses in judgment do not occur in the future.

Airlines are not the only travel industry taking the lead in gay and lesbian market segments. In 1993 Avis car rental and in 1994 National car rental both officially began waiving the additional driver fee for the partners of their gay and lesbian customers.

According to David Alport and Billy Kolber, who publish and edit *Out & About,* a gay and lesbian travel newsletter with a subscriber base of 9,500 (which actually implies a readership of at least 15,000 monthly): "[We] absolutely see all car rental companies moving toward this policy, basically because it makes sense. And this has come about because gay and lesbian consumers pushed for [it]. It's really a fairness issue. The important fact is, that it was the right thing to do."

However, according to editor Billy Kolber,

> Hertz has been fairly adamant in resisting this change. They claim it's a question of insurance liability and loss statistics. I think it's a party line [at Hertz]. . . . But [regarding the addition of the benefit] at Avis, they had just gone through an employee buyout, and as an employee-owned company they've become much more sensitive to customer issues. I predict Hertz will come around in the next few years. There is no way they can't.

David Alpert says,

> I think [as editors] on the car rental issue we haven't been anywhere near as vocal as we have been on the airline issue[s] . . . but we are [planning] more editorial coverage in this area, which will generate press. And now with two of the four companies having waived their policies, I think it's just going to take a push to drive the other two to follow.

Out & About recently gave Avis an editor's choice award based on their policy changes. They also released their first *Out & About Travel Guide* in association with Fodor's.

FUND-RAISING

There are hundreds of political and charitable gay and lesbian organizations across the United States representing tens of millions of dollars in grants, contributions, and in-kind services from gays, lesbians, and heterosexuals alike each year.

Currently no official national watchdog group monitors the affairs of these organizations other than their own boards and state reporting agencies. In some cases, in New York City, the annual reports of nonprofit groups are not made available to contributors, nor are many of these organizations held to any rigorous standard of accountability for their spending by the national gay and lesbian press.

A sampling of the total dollars contributed to just a few nonprofit organizations within the gay and lesbian community (prior to expenses) is as follows. This small snapshot of financial information in no way suggests that these organizations have mismanaged their funds; however, it has been provided since it represents a mere fraction of the total sum of revenue flowing annually among (and in many cases out of) the gay and lesbian community within the state of New York alone.

By looking at this information from earlier in the decade and comparing it to the budgets from the past year, the reader can begin to get an idea of just how many hundreds of millions of gay and lesbian philanthropic dollars are at stake in the coming years, as well as how small gay organization budgets are compared to more established ones. (Source: New York State Department of State Charities, Financial Summaries.)

Early 1990s Budgets

1991

Community Research Initiative	
Total support and revenue	$582,900

1992

Lambda Legal Defense and Education Fund	$1,619,294
Broadway Cares Inc.	
Total support and revenue	$1,994,520

1993

Minority Task Force on Aids	
Total support and revenue	$1,897,361
American Foundation for AIDS Research (AmFar)	
Total support and revenue 1991	$15,631,958
Total support and revenue 1992	20,646,721
Total support and revenue 1993	24,848,910
Total AmFar support/revenue past three years	$61,127,589

1997 Community Organization Budgets

Lesbian Herstory Archives	$42,000
PrideFest, Philadelphia	$120,000
ASTRAEA Foundation	$780,000
Horizons Center, Chicago	$1.2 million
Empire State Pride Agenda	$1.3 million
Gay & Lesbian Alliance Against Defamation (GLAAD)	$1.9 million
National Gay & Lesbian Task Force (NGLTF)	$2.5 million
Hetrick Martin Institute	$3.3 million
New York Lesbian & Gay Community Center	$3.8 million
God's Love We Deliver	$7.6 million
Human Rights Campaign (HRC)	$9.0 million
Los Angeles Gay and Lesbian Community Center	$19.0 million
AIDS Project Los Angeles (APLA)	$20.9 million
Gay Men's Health Crisis, New York City (GMHC)	$27.0 million
Public Broadcasting Corporation	$229.9 million
American Heart Association	$239.9 million
Boys & Girls Clubs of America	$302 million
Catholic Charities USA	$344.1 million
American Cancer Society	$359.1 million
YMCA	$361.2 million
United Jewish Appeal Federation	$408.2 million
Second Harvest	$430.6 million
CARE	$446 million
American Red Cross	$535.7 million
Salvation Army	$682.9 million

To alleviate even a question of impropriety or mismanagement, gay and lesbian nonprofit organizations should all make their annual financial summaries available upon request. The gay and lesbian press should take a stronger lead in holding these institutions accountable for their spending, political actions, and community program developments by publishing an analysis of their financial activity on an annual basis.

GAY AND LESBIAN BOOK, MAGAZINE, AND NEWSPAPER PUBLISHING

Gay and lesbian advertising in the gay and lesbian newspaper publishing industry is one of the brisker growth industries in the

entire gay and lesbian market spectrum. And it has long played a
role in the development of gay and lesbian local economies, creating a rallying and source point for gay and lesbian businesses,
consumers, readers, and community leaders to organize, communicate, reflect on political ideas, and exchange monies for goods and
services.

The sexual revolution of gay men clearly played an economic
role in the establishment and growth of gay and lesbian newspapers
and actually has its roots embedded in the historical actions of a few
courageous individuals dating back to the 1950s.

In an interview with one of the most important veteran gay activists in world history, Harry Hay (whom many regard as the father of
gay liberation), he explained what actually got the gay and lesbian
press going as an economically viable industry in the United States.
It involved the case of *ONE* magazine, a gay publication that had
been confiscated by the Los Angeles Postmaster as being obscene
because of its mere discussion of homosexuality.

Hay recalls:

> I suppose that undoubtedly the most major economic impact
> was our Supreme Court case because that case opened up all
> these public uses of the [United States] mails. This took us
> four years and several different [fights in court] to achieve
> that. But once that was achieved, virtually anything could be
> sent through the mail. Up until that time, the court had held
> that as an unstated policy, that the subject [homosexuality]
> could only be "discussed" [in print] in a medical, psychologi-
> cal, or religious point of view. You simply could not have a
> general discussion of homosexuality in a publicly printed
> piece going through the [United States] mail.
>
> That was *ONE* vs. Olson. Olson was the postmaster of LA
> who stopped our mail. We hauled him into court and charged
> him with violation of federal law.
>
> We made our point with a bang. And it automatically legis-
> lated for everyone in the then-forty-eight states. Our decision
> became the law, and no matter what anybody or any church
> thought, it is probably the most important civil rights case in
> our movement that has happened to date.

What it said was that our magazine [*ONE*] was not obscene. The Supreme Court laughed it out of the court. Dismissed it as utterly absurd.

In fact, even Kinsey was so upset about our case at the time, he was having things stopped by the postal inspector [as well]. He even came to LA to talk to us and ask us to withdraw our case because he was so afraid that it would jeopardize his case.

He thought he had a better case. We were this dinky little [group] in a ratty old downtown building, and he had a major institute with Rockefeller money behind him.

Our attorney was just a young law school graduate—hardly known, but then his phone started ringing from all over the country—Eric Julber.

From that time forward, more and more individuals began sending information, newsletters, and booklets through the mail, discussing issues of importance to lesbians and gay men.

Politics, sex, photographs, and various depictions of nudity in association with editorial copy were incorporated into publications and distributed through the mails. Eventually the distribution channels were extended to adult books and eventually some major newsstands with the help of *The Advocate* in the late 1970s.

Prior to 1990, every major nationally distributed gay or lesbian publication in the United States was forced to accept some kind of sexually oriented advertising in order to meet its business expenses. For at least fifteen years, much of the gay and lesbian press across the country was packed with some kind of advertising that was used as an excuse by larger, more mainstream advertisers for . . . not advertising. Whether it was phone sex, bathhouse, or personal classified advertisements, all were seen as inappropriate for the vast majority of display advertisers that had considered the gay and lesbian marketplace at one time or another.

Lambda Rising bookstore in Washington, DC, offers a comprehensive direct mail list totaling over 1,600 regularly produced gay and lesbian publications around the world. The entire list has a combined readership (circulation plus pass-along readers) of 16 million consumers.

About 300 of these publications are advertising-supported periodicals serving regional areas of the United States and Canada. In some American cities, there are more weekly gay and lesbian newspapers than there are mainstream news dailies.

In an independent survey conducted for this book of the 150 largest gay and lesbian news publications in the United States (response rate was 62 percent), the most common source of advertising revenue was independently owned bars, cabarets, restaurants, and discos. The second most common form of advertising was placed by local professional service firms such as attorneys, doctors, accountants, florists, carpet cleaning services, etc., most of which began publishing in the late 1970s and early 1980s.

Prior to 1989, there was not a single, nationally distributed publication with the words "gay and lesbian" on the cover—except the bold, controversial *Outweek* magazine. Not even *The Advocate* called itself a gay and lesbian publication until the pivotal installation of Richard Rouilard as editor in chief (in 1990)—whose stewardship alone may have been in reaction to the ever-more competitive nature of *Outweek* magazine.

Outweek was America's first nationally distributed gay and lesbian news weekly—a publication with women and people of color listed on its masthead, placed on its covers, and discussed between the covers more than any other publication of its kind. *Outweek* changed gay and lesbian news publishing in the United States forever. It shook up the New York editorial establishment and the entire gay and lesbian magazine wholesaling industry nationwide. Since then, a host of other gay and lesbian titles have appeared on the market.

In the words of former editor in chief Gabriel Rotello, "*Outweek* magazine provided a forum that helped to shape and crystalize the moment—for AIDS, for activism, and for a new generation of activists."

Former *Outweek* columnist Michelangelo Signorile says:

> *Outweek* magazine put so many issues on the front burner for the first time, so many issues that had not been discussed before—*Outweek* encouraged discussion, it pushed all issues out front, whether it was AIDS, health care, government, . . .

or outing. *Outweek* got the media to focus so much on gay and lesbian issues. It really was the voice of a new generation, a voice that was much more vocal, one that wasn't going to allow the media to keep [public figures] invisible. .

And when asked about outing . . .

> The word "outing" was something created by *Time* magazine. The word does a disservice to what we are talking about. We are talking about equalizing. Whenever sexuality is relevant [to a story in the media] it should be discussed. The same goes for homosexuality. It should be free to be discussed just like heterosexuality. [Americans] know everything about every public figure, do they have a husband, a wife, children? We [always] know that information when it comes to heterosexual public figures. Outing is simply about saying that there are times when homosexuality is very much about what an individual is saying—[especially] when they are [or are about to become] an elected public official. In that regard [*Outweek*] really did change much of the media. In fact, the media today has moved dramatically on this issue. We see a discussion of sexuality when it's relevant. . . . We now see public figures being asked if they are gay or lesbian . . .

Indeed, since *Outweek*, even *The New York Times* has commented on public officials who have been pressed on the issue of their sexual orientation. *The Advocate* outed former Pentagon spokesperson Pete Williams, which helped fuel the debate over gays and lesbians in the United States military.

Much of the tabloid press participated in outing a slew of Hollywood public figures, and newspapers began debating whether or not it was ethical to print the names of rape victims during prominent public trials. According to Signorile, even Dolly Parton was asked by a television reporter if she was a lesbian (she said "No, but so what if I was?").

Perhaps *Outweek*'s most controversial moment occurred when Malcom Forbes died. *Outweek* was the only publication to print an honest story about his life. The story was promoted like crazy (it was actually mailed to every television newsroom in the United States, creating an instantaneous media sensation).

With the publication of the Malcom Forbes story, newsstand circulation orders grew dramatically. Suddenly book chains were willing to distribute the magazine. Days earlier they weren't returning phone calls.

Money talks. A little hype doesn't hurt. More times than not it really helps. But to be all hype is nothing.

Outweek had substance, spirit, and character. It made people think. It made America talk and take positions. If not for *Outweek*, a number of prominent Hollywood figures might not have been exposed—might not have finally started rising to the times as their stature demanded (interestingly, their charitable donations to gay, lesbian, and AIDS-related organizations increased as well).

Outweek was revolutionary in other ways. Even its temporary experimentation with the removal of sexually oriented advertising raised eyebrows on Madison Avenue and heightened the sensitivity and appeal of other publications including *Genre,* which also successfully removed its sexually oriented advertising and is still publishing today.

Something special happened on West 25th at Seventh Avenue in New York City—during that short moment in gay and lesbian history, change occurred. Since that time, numerous efforts have been made to launch a publication in the New York City area for gay and lesbian consumers. New York writer Mark Schoofs attempted to start a newspaper for gays and lesbians in New York, but after much research came to the conclusion that it was, at least for him, not possible at the time. Schoofs comments, "Newspapers in general are risky to invest in. [We were] asking people to invest a sizable amount of money with the economy in bad shape . . . it was asking too much. We were able to raise 40 percent of what we needed. We raised $400,000—we were trying to raise a million."

Schoofs conducted a very extensive market research effort, looking at gay papers all over the country, but ultimately decided against the prospect.

Today there are more national gay and lesbian magazine publications in the United States than at any other time in history—all tucked into newsstands and drugstore shelves across America from New York City to shopping mall bookstores in Idaho—almost as common as apple pie.

Since the controversial publishing of Radcliffe Hall's *The Well of Loneliness* in 1928, an entire generation of gay and lesbian readers has passed through the world without ever experiencing the feeling of walking into a bookstore designed especially for them. Today there is a gay or lesbian bookstore in nearly every major American city in the United States. And literally hundreds of bookstores now stock titles under the specific heading of gay and lesbian studies.

Book publishing was extremely important to the lesbian movement. Barbara Grier, publisher of Naiad Press, remembers the days back in the 1950s when she was editing *The Ladder* for the Daughters of Bilitis. "We mimeographed it in the basement of Macy's on company time," she exclaims. Today, life is different for Grier. Her successful Naiad Press now grosses in excess of 1.5 million dollars annually and is currently paying royalties to over one hundred writers each year.

Barbara Grier says gay and lesbian book publishing is one of the single most important growth markets in all of gay and lesbian culture—indeed one of the most important in American mainstream culture as well.

In the 1950s and 1960s hundreds and hundreds of lesbian paperback novels were published—many of which were written by men for the erotic enjoyment of other men. As it turned out, many lesbians were attracted to the books and a literal revolution in lesbian political communication grew out of the phenomenon. This dynamic, combined with the underground women's music movement in the 1970s, had a strong economic effect on the ability of women to organize and share political ideas, emotions, and friendship through written and musical word.

Since the 1970s there has been an explosion of gay and lesbian book sales around the world, but it started primarily in the United States. In November 1967, the Oscar Wilde Bookstore opened in New York City. It was the first bookstore of its kind, stocking primarily gay- and lesbian-themed literature, nonfiction books, newspapers, and magazines. According to Bill Offenbaker, owner of Oscar Wilde Books, his sales are predominantly fiction, about 75 percent, to 25 percent nonfiction. "Women tend to buy more paperback murder mysteries, men tend to buy the hardcovers, both fiction and nonfiction." The bookshop currently stocks over 10,000 titles. He has also noticed an increase in the purchasing of relationship books among men: "It happens every spring," he says. "I've noticed now for the past few years."

In 1979, A Different Light Books opened on the West Coast in the Silverlake section of Los Angeles. A Different Light eventually opened a store in New York City in 1983, in San Francisco in 1986, and West Hollywood in 1990. Most recently, A Different Light closed its store in West Greenwich Village, moving a few blocks uptown to the growing Chelsea area of Manhattan.

Norman Laurila, owner, and Roz Parr, general manager, claimed that business had grown so much in the New York store that people could hardly move on the weekends. The Different Light on Hudson Street was also small (only 800 sq. feet). Their new store on Nineteenth Street has four times the room. A Different Light's expansion is a particularly telling commentary on the extraordinary growth of the gay and lesbian book publishing industry—most of which occurred in the 1980s—as well as the shift in gay and lesbian population density in New York and Los Angeles.

A key hallmark of A Different Light is the fact that they keep nearly every gay and lesbian book in print stocked in their stores—currently over 15,000 titles. Roz Parr believes that the overall inventory of gay and lesbian-themed books in A Different Light, combined with books of gay and lesbian interest, could possibly approach 25,000 by the year 2000.

Most gay and lesbian bookstores report that 70 to 85 percent of their sales are in books, with the remainder comprising magazines, newspapers, and journals. (Of those stores carrying erotic magazine products, most claimed at least 50 percent of their overall magazine sales to be in the erotic category—predominately male-oriented.)

Jed Mattes, a literary agent since 1975, has represented a wide range of authors, many of whom are gay or lesbian, including the late Vito Russo, author of *The Celluloid Closet*. He believes the market will continue to grow as well, but will become more and more diversified. Discussions with other book editors and publishing agents in New York City reveal somewhat parallel thinking regarding the future of the gay and lesbian publishing market.

Mattes comments:

> There are certain [publishing] houses that are more likely than others to [publish a gay or lesbian book] but I don't think there is one house that I would say, "No don't send it to them; they won't buy."
>
> There are some houses that are unlikely but not because they are hostile. I think some houses just don't have a sales force that is as knowledgeable as some others, or they don't have editors that are [thinking necessarily in those terms].

Deacon Maccubbin, owner of the Lambda Rising Bookstore in Washington, DC, believes he could easily have a total stock of over 20,000 different gay and lesbian titles by the year 2000. He predicts this is due "in large part because there are so many more gay [and lesbian] people coming out and more and more straight people interested in gay-themed books—especially straight people who work with gay people, which is an increasingly large number of people all the time. We have always had a substantial straight clientele since we opened in 1974."

The bookstore's catalog goes to over 500,000 people between second class mailings and inserts in regionally distributed gay and lesbian news publications. Advertising is also now available in the catalog as well. Interestingly, Lambda Rising's best mail-order customers predominate in Texas and Florida. Deacon claims mail-order customers from those two states buy more books than anywhere else in the country.

Currently, there are over 175 gay and lesbian bookstores in the United States, 145 lesbian feminist bookstores, and probably over 500 general interest bookstores with gay and lesbian book sections (a trend that has developed over the last ten years).

Overall the market's future appears to be heading in a direction of continued but somewhat slower growth and more diversification with books focusing on humor, entertainment, community analysis, and changing gay and lesbian culture. A key theme is the desire of individual gays and lesbians to become more involved in their own personal interests and communities—many wanting to know how they can become more a part of the overall gay and lesbian culture.

A number of bookstore managers claim gay and lesbian customers have a strong need to know what is happening in the national community and how one can get involved in helping to empower the national gay and lesbian political process.

The exploding gay and lesbian publishing world is allowing a new generation of gays and lesbians to celebrate their sexuality and spirit—especially in areas of the country where gay and lesbian culture is not as defined, open, or progressive. Trends over the next few years in gay and lesbian book sales will undoubtedly reflect changes in gay and lesbian culture.

In the late 1970s and early 1980s sales agents often complained that they couldn't get retail bookstores to stock gay and lesbian titles. Times have clearly changed.

MEDIA, ADVERTISING, AND DIRECT MARKETING

As mentioned, the best mailing list rentals available for self-identifying gay and lesbian consumers currently come from Strubco in New York City, regional gay and lesbian news publications and subscription services, a few regional gay and lesbian bookstores, national glossy magazines, private membership clubs, some nonprofit groups, and increasingly, individual gay and lesbian-owned retail businesses.

Using direct marketing as a way of reaching the gay and lesbian market is not only effective, but a smart way to test the waters for companies who are considering marketing to gays and lesbians for the first time. The use of direct marketing also allows for more disclosure regarding language and imagery when marketing to gays and lesbians—language and imagery some marketers may fear incorporating into a magazine or outdoor vehicle. The direct marketing examples from AT&T and American Express given earlier illustrate the varying approaches that have been applied to direct marketing efforts for different gay and lesbian market segments.

Rather than attempting to catalog what is now easily more than twenty-five sizable gay and lesbian marketing, advertising, and public relations specialty firms nationwide, who their clients are, and what their professional relationships are becoming within the emerging gay and lesbian media business, I've opted instead to include a sampling of a variety of campaigns (see photo insert) that have been launched over the past couple of years. In addition, there is a listing of important gay and lesbian business and consumer organizations in Appendix A that can be consulted for more information regarding gay/lesbian-owned firms.

A sampling of what some of America's more involved and out gay and lesbian market pioneers are thinking is worth mentioning, as are a few remarks and insights I recorded in interviews with key gay and lesbian marketplace thinkers.

Two advertising industry professionals on Madison Avenue, Mark Horn, a senior copywriter and vice president with Wunderman Cato Johnson, and Nancy Webster, a creative director at Burson Marsteller, offered insights surrounding the shrewdness of IKEA's recent foray into gay and lesbian target marketing, a television commercial of a gay male couple buying home furnishings.

"I was shocked at the IKEA ad," intoned Horn. "They spent money [targeting] the community and it got out in the world at large in a way that had a political effect that all my years of political activism never had. Although, years of activism may ultimately have led IKEA to do it. But [that combination] in its own way is very important, very supportive. I will always give money and my business to people who support me, I will certainly not give my money to Cracker Barrel restaurants [see Chapter 5] or to people who want to burn me at the stake."

The advertisement no doubt broke new ground and earned IKEA much publicity and an award from GLAAD, but some gay and lesbian marketing professionals noted that the advertisement showed only men, which surely had to annoy more than a few lesbian shoppers. Especially since there's no definitive data that lesbians buy fewer midpriced dining tables than gay men do.

Nancy Webster perceived the IKEA advertising as a shrewd and insightful example illustrative of how much advertising relies on sending a variety of messages to a variety of different consumer groups, commenting, " 'Gay' connotes men, you use the word gay, so you're talking about men. It's almost easier for women to pass; you have less of an idea of difference. One of the reasons that some gay women are not out at work is because they really can pass more easily than gay men. If a woman is living alone or with a family member, nobody thinks that much about that, but if it's an older man living with his brother, people think about it and wonder. It goes back to this idea of difference—two women shopping together is typical, two men shopping together is different.

"It's been my experience that many heterosexual women love gay men. I think that straight women love gay men more than they love lesbians. I don't think they have a problem with lesbians, but I think that IKEA was thinking about straight women."

"Advertising reduces people to markets and people in advertising to objects," acknowledges Horn. "And inasmuch as gay people are becoming more a part of society, gay culture and gay men and women are experiencing equal opportunity exploitation. It will be interesting to see how lesbians do or do not become objectified in advertising in years to come."

Direct marketing is also especially risk-free in terms of potential backlash. It's a low-profile, highly targeted medium allowing versatility in segmentation and an excellent opportunity for a company to begin building its own database of gay and lesbian customers.

Sean Strub of Metamorphics Media in New York City offers a large selection of gay and lesbian lists—some of which are his own and others that are simply managed by his firm. Among all lists available from Metamorphics Media, ten top interests and activities run as a theme among gay and lesbian donor and prospect names that may be of particular interest to new direct marketers. They are:

- Art/antique collecting
- Cultural/art events
- Donating and volunteering to charitable groups
- Foreign travel
- Gourmet cooking/fine foods
- Owning a CD player
- Personal home computing
- Physical fitness, sports, and exercise activities
- Buying CDs and tapes
- Fine wines

Gay- and lesbian-owned agencies, or agencies specializing in gay and lesbian advertising and media, are growing rapidly across the United States. This trend can be expected to continue over the next ten years as more and more gay and lesbian markets diversify and start requiring more specialized service providers in regional markets.

CHANGES YET TO COME

Spectacular opportunities exist for automobile sales as well as products, parts, and service maintenance companies among gays and lesbians in the United States. Nearly every gay or lesbian consumer in the United States who has a driver's license (and doesn't live in New York City, but including many of them) drives an automobile.

Considering how brand-loyal gays and lesbians are, there would be no easier way to immediately increase domestic car sales even more than the record numbers posted throughout this decade, than for the big three automakers to simply target a slice of their advertising to the gay and lesbian consumer automotive markets.

Although numerous regional dealerships have successfully advertised to gay and lesbian consumers through regional area publications, it took the import manufacturers Saab, Volkswagen, and Subaru to take the plunge, becoming the first to target gay and lesbian Americans through the pages of *OUT* magazine and, some say, a commercial (Volkswagen) that ran during *Ellen's* coming-out episode.

In the meantime, insurance companies and financial services companies have begun aggressively targeting gay and lesbian consumers—particularly American Express and Hartford Insurance. The same can be said for some medical and pharmaceutical companies, which have installed domestic partner health care coverage (although several also have yet to incorporate that change despite brisk sales of AIDS-related drugs).

"Any pharmaceutical or biotech company investing money in AIDS research now views [meeting with the consumer] as a must," according to David Gold, a writer and former director of the medical information program at GMHC (Gay Men's Health Crisis) in New York City, the nation's oldest and largest AIDS service organization. Gold states that:

. . . as soon as AIDS began impacting people's lives—around the mid-1980s—the stakes were so high that gays and lesbians—but predominantly gay men—started creating huge organizations in their communities. First you had big social service industries developing within the gay community, which had never happened before. Than you had gay people learning everything about the pharmaceutical industry—which eventually changed patient care across the country. Now we have openly gay patient care advocates at the highest levels of the medical establishment [in the United States]. Now you see major businesses targeting people with AIDS or HIV. It has come full circle with companies now viewing gays in the medical fields as important and informed consumers.

In the beginning these companies did not want to have anything to do with activists, then ACT UP [AIDS Coalition to Unleash Power] got into the headquarters of Burroughs Wellcome and barricaded themselves in their offices until they would listen.

Today medical companies actively pursue these activists. Companies now fly me and [other activists] out to their headquarters to see if we think the drug approval process is coming along properly. We basically now [strategize together and share information] to get drugs approved more rapidly.

You now see this [phenomenon developing] with breast cancer and prostate cancer advocacy groups. And these [new activists are taking their cues] by virtue of what they witnessed happening with AIDS activism in the gay community.

I don't think it would be an understatement at all to say that the way the gay community has dealt with AIDS has transformed the American health care industry. The doctor-patient relationship has been forever altered. In many cases, AIDS and cancer patients now know more than the doctors—that has never happened in the history of medicine.

David Gold's words should be heeded by all large companies that hope to sell products and services to gays and lesbians. While it is true that AIDS activism bears the reality and urgency of life and death and time's passage through history, as we approach the next presidential election tension continues to build among gay and lesbian consumer enclaves across the United States—both within and outside of large corporate establishments.

Gay and lesbian consumers are simply going to continue to flex their financial and organizational muscle. And business can only profit by incorporating them into the process—as an ally—in much the same way the medical field has had to learn to do.

Chapter 7

The Future of the Gay and Lesbian Marketplace: Considerations at the Door of the Twenty-First Century

We didn't talk for about four months, [then] we had a long two-hour meeting in the Oval Office. We've agreed to disagree [on the military issue] while still working [together] in other areas. It was a private meeting; we both agreed not to talk about it.

David Mixner
A personal friend of President Clinton
for the past twenty-five years

Imagine for a moment a world in which the majority of the global population is born gay or lesbian. In such a society, less than 10 percent of the total population would be heterosexuals. In the United States alone, citizens would accord themselves individual rights and economic privileges based on laws, customs, and historical precedent related to their sexual orientation, their view of the world, and basic experience as gay and lesbian people.

In this virtually all gay and lesbian world, let's pretend that heterosexuals are largely ignored, because the gay and lesbian masses largely regard heterosexuals as a confused people with complicated social and sexual problems. Some believe the heterosexuals to be immoral. Some of the allegedly more enlightened elements within the gay and lesbian majority argue that heterosexuals are not immoral but sick, and should therefore be pitied or "tolerated."

In time, attitudes change. Heterosexual acts are decriminalized. Some states begin to allow heterosexuals to adopt children. And a few leading businesses begin treating them as legitimate workers and consumers worthy of good products and good job protections.

Eventually, the public begins to think that maybe they should be given equal workplace rights, but most maintain and argue that heterosexuals should not be given any special rights or status as a minority group.

TIMES ARE A-CHANGING

History will recall the end of the twentieth century as the turning point in gay and lesbian emancipation in America. It may also recall the last half of the twentieth century as the bittersweet golden years of American gay and lesbian culture. It is a time for gay and lesbian people filled with promise, social progress, and economic momentum bringing legitimacy and status to themselves and their families as an important new minority of people.

But history will also underline the never-ending grief, shame, castigation, and hypocrisy surrounding AIDS, AIDS funding, and AIDS education that cowardly political elements within America's culture heaped upon gay and lesbian individuals.

As gay and lesbian culture expands, it also becomes more fragmented yet dichotomously stronger because of that fragmentation. As Alan Roskoff, assistant to New York Public Advocate Mark Greene, comments:

> I meet people who are openly gay and assume that we have a lot in common politically and then I find out they are gay Republicans. . . . Twenty years ago when I met people active in the gay movement, they were anti-war activists by and large, not people I would find myself on opposite sides of the aisle with, arguing over economic issues or race relations. I think [politicians such as] Guiliani [have] a typical Republican mentality, and part of the agenda is not to take care of those who need to be taken care of the most or need help the most. It's a policy of writing off the most defenseless. I think the lesbian and gay community does not have a friend in [people like that] even if on certain issues [they] pass a certain litmus test—they're still Republican first, and therefore issues and economics are not going to be pleasing a community that cares about AIDS, the homeless, and others [who are at a disadvantage].

Today, gay and lesbian people's status within American culture is marked by constitutional and legal uncertainty, and numerous profound moral and political questions remain. As the clock ticks louder and louder with the issues surrounding gay and lesbian emancipation at the government level, business continues to surge ahead.

The movement for equal rights of gay and lesbian Americans is simply an issue whose time has come. It is a time when we should all be asking ourselves whether we are going to allow liberty and democracy to endure and extend to all Americans regardless of age, sex, race, ethnicity, creed, religion, *and sexual orientation*, or if we are going to allow ourselves to put limits on our interpretation of what a free society can be in the twenty-first century.

The gay and lesbian emancipation movement has unveiled the cowardice of the world's toughest generals in United States Department of Defense. It has rattled the office of the president. It has challenged judges, clergy, police officers, and national spokespeople from Dade County, Florida, to the private papal recesses of the Vatican. It is not going to go away.

In some ways, the legitimacy of one's sexual orientation as a social, political, economic, and spiritual identity is a moot point that can no longer be debated; it already exists in reality, at every level of society. Gay and lesbian sexuality is not a lifestyle; it is a life fact.

As the issues surrounding that certitude continue to be fought in city councils, statehouses, and school board meetings across America, some of the brightest hope for change and leadership is coming from our corporate boardrooms and marketing planning committees.

Business cannot wait. And in business gay and lesbian Americans have a friend, and, conversely, so does business have the opportunity to have a friend in gay and lesbian consumerism.

The time to take action is now. America's best businesses will see and take advantage of the opportunity for change, growth, and social renewal that is related to their partnering with the gay and lesbian consumer revolution in America. They also recognize that their competition is no longer immune to the issues surrounding gay and lesbian freedoms—both in the courtrooms and the marketplace.

American business does not have to become a forum where gay and lesbian political battles are fought. If American business wants to avoid the coming battles surrounding that debate, it will side with gay and lesbian people—as individuals, as employees, and as consumers—as Americans. Businesses need only seek to support gay and lesbian individuality both in their treatment of individuality and labor, and in their recognition of gay and lesbian consumption.

The gay and lesbian consumer revolution is born of informed, organized individuals who are realizing that their fight for human rights is now becoming an economic process as much as it has been a political process—a new cultural dynamism of identity.

To support equal rights for gay and lesbian Americans is really to join in the ongoing fight for the protection of everyone's individual rights. The business leaders who are taking a stand and establishing or reaffirming their commitment to gay and lesbian emancipation are taking a stand for their own economic prosperity as well. You can't have free enterprise without free individuals.

In the final analysis, businesses that support the call for stronger protection of individual liberties—regardless of sexual orientation—will be the ones that establish themselves as leaders among America's emerging national family of gay and lesbian consumers. If businesses truly believe that ultimately the customer is always right, regardless of sexual orientation, then they need only listen, provide the goods, and reap the benefits: a talented workforce, a greater profit margin, and more competitive products and services.

The Gay Games held in New York City in 1994 made clear to the world that gay and lesbian people are going to go on living their lives and developing their own communities, their own institutions of pride and sustenance. It is a bittersweet time in American politics—both socially and economically—for gays and lesbians as well as heterosexuals. In a perfect world, there would be no need for a Gay Games, Gay Pride, or perhaps even a gay and lesbian marketplace.

But in a perfect world, Brenda and Wanda Henson of Camp Sister Spirit would be able to run their private women's retreat in Mississippi without having to suffer at the hands of bigots. They would be able to buy gravel and supplies without being faced with restraint of trade issues all across the county. Attorney General

Janet Reno had to send federal marshals in to attempt to bring an end to the crisis of harassment that Brenda and Wanda continually faced from the surrounding community.

In a perfect world Camp Sister Spirit wouldn't have to fight in court to apply United States Code 241, known as the anticlan act, to get, as Wanda Henson exclaims in a broken voice, "the neighbors to leave us alone [for being lesbians]—this is why we need a civil rights law to protect gays and lesbians. I don't mind putting my ass on the line like this but I need help. [It frightens me that] a cow farmer that was selling hay to [us], was ordered by neighbors [to] stop. [When he didn't], two of his calves were shot. The Justice Department attorneys told us, 'We're sorry but there are no civil rights laws to protect you, none for gays and lesbians.' I asked how can this be [in America]?"

Camp Sister Spirit represents more than homophobia, more than bigotry—it symbolizes the ongoing fight against the unfair economic practices and social policies that are largely unaddressed at this late date in democratic history.

But Harold Levine, director of marketing for the Gay Games in 1994, paints the picture of a road filled with hope, headed toward change, prosperity, and goodwill for both American business and gay and lesbian people everywhere when he comments:

> In retrospect, the Gay Games marked the point when marketers stopped asking whether they should market to the gay and lesbian community and started asking how they should reach this marketplace. Mainstream sponsors reaped enormous benefits from the games. A mail survey conducted ten weeks after the games by the Gay Games organizing committee found unaided recall of over 35 percent for Naya Bottled Water, Miller Beer, and AT&T, twice what a mainstream event sponsorship could be expected to bring. And the games also laid to rest widespread fears of a right-wing backlash. Mainstream sponsors were highly visible, and the press covered the involvement of Miller Beer, Continental Airlines, Naya Water, and AT&T in depth. There was no backlash. What sponsors did find was an enormous gratitude among gay men and lesbians—that they had supported an event so important to gay

and lesbian people across the United States—in fact, around the world.

Since the Gay Games in 1994, countless American businesses, large and small, have implemented written nondiscrimination policy statements, domestic partner health insurance benefits, and well-executed gay and lesbian target marketing initiatives.

As more companies compete for more gay customers, the expansion of the gay consumer market phenomenon will continue until it has reached nearly every industry sector possible. It is already bringing more cultural awareness, equality, and respect for others in the workplace, it is opening new opportunities in the marketplace, and it is resulting in better business practices for everyone—from Wall Street to Main Street.

And as every good business leader knows, the customer is always right.

Appendix A

Independent Information Sources for Gay- and Lesbian-Oriented Advertisers and Marketers

Council on Economic Priorities
30 Irving Place
New York, NY 10003
(212) 420-1133

Equality Project
185 East 85th Street, Suite 25A
New York, NY 10028-2147
(212) 870-2296

Gay and Lesbian Alliance Against Defamation
150 West 26th Street #503
New York, NY 10001
(212) 807-1700

Human Rights Campaign Fund
P.O. Box 1396
Washington, DC 20013
(202) 628-4160

National Association of People with AIDS
1413 K Street, NW, 7th Floor
Washington, DC 20005
(202) 898-0414

National Gay and Lesbian Task Force
2320 17th Street, NW
Washington, DC 20009
(202) 332-6483

New York Advertising and Communications Network
Box 149
332 Bleeker Street
New York, NY 10014-2980
24-hour message line: (212) 517-0380

Appendix B

A Note on Yankelovich MONITOR's Sensitivity Techniques

In an effort to provide a broad picture of what is going on in the minds of American consumers, the Yankelovich MONITOR covers a wide variety of subjects, many of them extremely sensitive. In order to ensure accurate information on these issues, Yankelovich has constructed a number of research techniques to alleviate embarrassment or anxiety on the respondent's part.

Two are particularly worth noting again because of their relationship to the gay and lesbian sample participants and those that responded as gay, lesbian, or homosexual:

- The 1½-hour questionnaire is administered in the respondent's home—a secure environment controlled by the respondent.
- Sensitive topics, such as those dealing with individual identity, are placed in a spiral binder of exhibit cards. For such questions, each respondent is instructed to turn to the appropriate card and asked to indicate only the numbers of the responses they choose. In this way, respondents disclose information confidentially.

Further, each individual is scored based upon responses to a series of questions. Scores are used for two primary reasons:

- Tracking from years past to determine the size and direction of social change
- To compare and contrast two or more groups in order to gain insight into the motivations and needs of one group versus another

IDENTIFICATION OF A SCIENTIFICALLY RELEVANT
GAY/LESBIAN SAMPLE

The highly accurate scientific sample of gay/lesbian respondents identified for this study was obtained by means of an item in the 1994 Yankelovich MONITOR's questionnaire that asked participants to choose from a descriptive list of fifty-two adjectives/phrases that describe them. One of the fifty-two descriptors was "gay/lesbian/homosexual."

The information contained in the following data represents approximately 6 percent of the 2,503 respondents, sixteen years of age and older (n = 148), who indicated that "gay/lesbian/homosexual" described them. This sophisticated self-identification technique is significantly more reliable than others used to analyze the gay/lesbian population in the past.

Population samples made up of magazine, catalog, and direct-marketing subscription lists—or of those who voluntarily return mail questionnaires—are neither random nor representative of the population as a whole. By their very nature they contain substantial bias because they only represent those consumers. Yet, in no way does this disparage the value of using information or lists culled from various marketing companies—even if their methods of obtaining names rely heavily on convenience sampling. It is important to know in placing media what a specific magazine's readers are like, or what a specific marketing company's lists or panel of participants is like. But that information is only representative of those publications and marketing company panels, and cannot be accurately extrapolated to the population as a whole.

Notes

Chapter 1

1. Lukenbill, Grant (1995). *Untold millions: Positioning your business for the gay and lesbian consumer revolution.* New York: HarperCollins, p. 1.

2. See Russo, Vito (1981). *The celluloid closet.* New York: Harper & Row.

3. Shilts, Randy (1993). *Conduct unbecoming: Gays and lesbians in the U.S. military.* New York: St. Martin's Press, p. 15.

4. Roger Ricklefs (1995, May 1). Big business boosts efforts to win share of gay market. *The Wall Street Journal,* Enterprise section, p. 1.

5. West, Cornel (1993). *Race matters.* Boston: Beacon, p. 25.

6. Larson, Erik (1992). *The naked consumer: How our private lives become public commodities.* New York: Henry Holt & Co., p. 68.

Chapter 2

1. Edelman, Murray (1994). The gay and lesbian vote and estimates of population size, prepared for presentation at the annual meeting of the American Statistical Association. Contact the Voter News Service, 225 West 34th Street Suite 310, New York, NY 10022 for a complete copy. Telephone (212) 947-7280; fax (212) 947-7756.

2. The Yankelovich MONITOR is an ongoing research project conducted annually (since 1971) by Yankelovich Partners. The underlying methodological assumption is that traditional economic and demographic predictors are insufficient for a complete understanding of marketplace behavior. In addition to measuring the traditional demographics, MONITOR is designed to quantitatively measure social attitudes, values, and perceptions, thus sketching a complete portrait of the consumer.

3. *Time*/CNN News, June 15-16, 1994, conducted by Yankelovich MONITOR, 101 Marritt 7 Corporate Park, Norwalk, Connecticut 06851.

4. See Murdoch (1994, May 24). *The New York Times,* Section 4, p. 1

5. See Faludi, Susan (1991). *Backlash: The undeclared war against American women.* New York: Crown.

6. *Life* (1964). Homosexuality in America. June 26, p. 76.

7. Welch, Paul (1964). The gay world takes to the streets. *Life,* June 26, p. 68.

8. *The Wall Street Journal,* May 13, 1975, More Businesses Targeting Homosexuals.

Chapter 3

1. In addition to the need for random probability sampling, there are other challenges that researchers face when conducting research on sexual behavior and sexual identity in human beings. These include: making allowances for errors and distortions that can occur when respondents refuse to answer certain questions or proceed to withhold important information for undisclosed reasons; making allowances for participants who respond to questions the way they think they should rather than expressing their understanding of the actual truth; or when a respondent answers a question erroneously to cover for what is perceived to be a trick question or could lead to criminal prosecution.

All of these issues are faced by researchers—but they become especially important when conducting sexual research because of societal taboos, insecurity about one's own sexual behavior, or simply embarrassment over the discussion and consideration of the subject of sexuality itself.

For these reasons, it is nearly impossible to conduct a definitive study that will conclusively determine how many people there are who are actually gay or lesbian.

But sexual behavior alone simply does not determine sexual identity. As has been stated, all that really matters for marketing purposes is determining the number of individuals in a given geographic area who are willing to self-identify as gay or lesbian—people who are willing to be counted as "being gay or lesbian" in a scientific study—regardless of their sexual behavior. By knowing this number first, marketers are provided with an extremely conservative estimate from which to make assumptions about the overall prospective marketplace and growth potentials.

The point? Studies of sexual behavior tell us about just that: sexual behavior—which is radically different from consumer behavior. While it is true that some studies can arrive at general quantitative assumptions based on the consistency or exclusivity of sexual behavior, we are, again, only talking about sexual behavior. Segmenting advertising campaigns and marketing programs toward prospective gay and lesbian consumers requires more than relying on the same tired scientifically quantified sexual behavior estimates cranked out by various universities and think tanks.

Sexual behavioral studies telling us how many people are having what kind of sex in a given geographic area are of little importance or use to businesspeople wanting to make an honest buck by conducting legitimate business with America's gay and lesbian consumer populations.

Marketing studies that tell us how many people in a geographic area are willing to discuss their values, hopes, fears, wants, and needs while also self-identifying as being gay or lesbian tell us much more.

Fortunately, more and more marketing studies based on gay and lesbian identity are now being conducted and reported. And fewer and fewer behavioral studies on sexuality are being accepted as relevant to modern marketing science.

2. Badgett, Lee (1995). The wage effect of sexual orientation. *Industrial Labor Relations Review,* July.

3. The Rand Report to the U.S. Military (Contract No. MDA903-90-C-0004) was prepared for the Office of the Secretary of Defense (at the time Les Aspin) by the Rand Corporation. It totaled over 500 pages and detailed major U.S. probability studies that it found to be conducted under sound scientific methodology. Rand is a nonprofit institution that seeks to improve public policy through research and analysis. Publications of Rand do not necessarily reflect the opinions or policies of the sponsors of Rand research.

4. Pomeroy, Wardell B. (1972). *Dr. Kinsey and the Institute for Sex Research.* New York: Harper & Row, p. 3.

5. Ibid., p. 111.

6. Ibid., p. 112.

7. Janus, Samuel S. (1994). *Janus report on sexual behavior.* New York: John Wiley.

8. John O. Billy et al. (1992). The sexual behavior of men in the United States. *Family Planning Perspective 25:* 52. *Family Planning Perspective* is published by The Alan Guttmacher Institute, 111 Fifth Avenue, New York, NY 10003.

9. The Profile of the NGNG readership is the exclusive property of the National Gay Newspaper Guild. No use or quotation of this study from its contents may be made by anyone without the permission of a guild member or an authorized representative.

10. This report does not reflect data from *The New York Blade* which did not begin publishing until November 1997.

11. Employee spoke on condition of anonymity.

12. See Chapter 2, note 1.

13. National Opinion Research Center (1992). *The National Health and Social Life Survey.* Chicago: University of Chicago.

14. *Newsweek* (February 14, 1994). Homophobia, politics, and issues.

15. Reprinted with permission from The Human Rights Campaign, Washington, DC.

16. There has been some argument in academic circles over whether responses to sexual inquiries can become suppressed or elevated during such research interviews—particularly those dealing with issues of homosexuality.

Some studies, such as those cited in Rand (see Chapter 2), used a self-administered questionnaire requiring the participant to actually "divulge on paper" the nature of some of their most intimate sexual feelings; other studies have used face-to-face interviews, which still required the participants to verbally say, discuss, or otherwise disclose their sexual identity.

The Yankelovich technique is unique in that a spiral binder of exhibit cards allows each respondent to simply flip through fifty-two different cards and indicate only the numbers on the cards that correspond to statements or words that best describe them; one of the cards is labeled gay/lesbian/homosexual.

This may seem only subtly different from choosing a box on an anonymous paper questionnaire or verbally making a yes or no statement to an interviewer. But as described in the previous chapter, when you consider the degree to which most homosexual persons have either been a victim of, or are familiar with, the way the church, the state, and the medical establishment have treated homosexuality, I argue that any respondent would be suspicious of such a question no matter how it was put to them.

I believe the very act of checking off a box on a paper questionnaire about homosexuality has its own perceived implications in the subconscious of the respondent—as would stating the fact verbally.

The paper questionnaire leaves a paper trail; the face-to-face interview requires that the respondent actually state his or her orientation or to say the words gay, lesbian or homosexual. Subconsciously, many gay or lesbian respondents might perceive the requirement to answer such a question as a confession of what society has traditionally characterized as a "perversion," "sickness," or "crime" (whether they believed it was really an anonymous or confidential question or not).

Yankelovich's approach, at least on this issue, reduces the fear of the respondent much more, allowing a greater comfort level with the divulgence of sexual identity. The respondent is not left with the feeling that a paper trail has been left behind.

I emphasize this issue because I believe that a window of security has been provided through the spiral binder approach, and that it has actually identified more gay and lesbian people in the population than previous, perhaps less sophisticated, studies have indicated. In fact, it may be that, through this process, some respondents actually acknowledged to themselves for the very first time that they indeed are as the chart indicated: "gay/lesbian/homosexual."

Chapter 4

1. Pomeroy, Wardell B. (1972). *Dr. Kinsey and the Institute for Sex Research.* New York: Harper & Row, p. 273.

2. Yankelovich MONITOR 1994.

3. National Public Radio (January 16, 1994). *All Things Considered.*

4. *The New York Times* (May 30, 1995). p. A5.

5. Population Council (May 30, 1995). Families in focus.

6. Thompson, Mark (1994). *Gay soul: Interviews and photographs.* San Francisco, CA: HarperSanFrancisco.

7. Gilfoyle, Timothy J. (1994). *City of Eros: New York City, prostitution, and the commercialization of sex, 1790-1920.* New York: W.W. Norton, pp. 19, 30, 98-99, 254.

8. D'Emilio, John (1983). *Sexual politics, sexual communities: The making of a homosexual minority in the United States 1940-1970.* Chicago: University of Chicago Press, pp. 19, 247.

9. Gore, Al (1992). *Earth in the balance: Ecology and the human spirit.* Boston: Houghton Mifflin.

10. From the Social Climate Overview of the 1993 Yankelovich MONITOR. It is intended to provide a broad contextual understanding of significant trends for the total population. It is part of a focused analysis of the gay/lesbian population in the Yankelovich MONITOR Gay and Lesbian Perspective conducted originally

for this book with the intention of comparing such trends among self-identifying gay and lesbian individuals to the total population.

11. Badgett, Lee (1995, July). The wage effects of sexual orientation discrimination. *Industrial Labor Relations Review.*

Chapter 5

1. Popcorn, Faith (1991). *The Popcorn report.* New York: HarperBusiness, p. 162.

2. The Wall Street Project (1993). Equality principles on sexual orientation.

3. Winfeld, Liz and Spielman, Sue (1994). *Straight talk about gays in the workplace.* New York: AMACOM.

4. Mickens, Ed (1994). *The 100 best companies for gay men and lesbians.* New York: Pocket Books; Strub, Sean, Baker, Dan, and Henning, Bill (1994). *Cracking the corporate closet.* New York: HarperBusiness.

5. Friskopp, Annette and Silverstein, Sharon (1995). *Straight jobs, gay lives.* New York: Simon and Schuster.

6. Mickens, Ed. (April 19, 1994). Waging war on Wall Street. *The Advocate,* p. 41.

7. *The Miami Herald* (1997). See note 9.

8. *The Nation* (April 15, 1978). p. 434.

9. Bellant, Russ (1988). *The Coors connection: How Coors family philanthropy undermines democratic pluralism.* Boston: South End Press.

10. Mickens, *The 100 best companies for gay men and lesbians,* Introduction.

11. Strub, Baker, and Henning, *Cracking the corporate closet,* Introduction.

12. *The Wall Street Journal* (May 13, 1975).

13. *The Wall Street Journal* (May 13, 1975). Campaigns to sell to homosexual market are being launches by more big firms.

Chapter 6

1. *The New York Times* (September 6, 1994). Gay presence leads revival of declining neighborhoods.

Bibliography

Altman, Dennis (1982). *The homosexualization of America: The Americanization of the homosexual.* New York: St. Martin's Press.

Badgett, Lee (1995, July). The wage effects of sexual orientation discrimination. *Industrial Labor Relations Review.*

Baker, Dan, Henning, Bill, and Strub, Sean (1995). *Cracking the corporate closet.* New York: HarperBusiness.

Bawer, Bruce (1993). *A place at the table.* New York: Poseidon Press.

Bellant, Russ (1988). *The Coors connection: How Coors family philanthropy undermines democratic pluralism.* Boston: South End Pres.

Bérubé, Allan (1990). *Coming out under fire: The history of gay men and women in World War Two.* New York: Free Press.

Billy, John O. et al. (1992). The sexual behavior of men in the United States. *Family Planning Perspective 25: 52.*

Boswell, John (1980). *Christianity, social tolerance, and homosexuality: Gay people in Western Europe from the beginning of the Christian Era to the fourteenth century.* Chicago: University of Chicago Press.

Browning, Frank (1993). *Culture of desire.* New York: Crown.

Brun, Bernard (1991). *The timetables of history.* New Third Revised Edition (based upon Werner Stein's *Kulturfahrplan*). Touchstone, Simon and Schuster.

Chauncey, George (1994). *Gay New York: Gender, urban culture, and the making of the gay male world 1890-1940.* New York: HarperCollins, 1994.

Chilton, John (1975). *Billie's blues.* New York: Stein and Day/Scarborough House.

Cohen, Dorothy (1981). *Consumer behavior.* New York: Random House.

D'Emilio, John (1983). *Sexual politics, sexual communities: The making of a homosexual minority in the United States, 1940-1970.* Chicago: University of Chicago Press.

D'Emilio, John, and Freedman, Estelle B. (1988). *Intimate matters: A history of sexuality in America.* New York: Harper & Row.

Duberman, Martin (1993). *Stonewall.* New York: Dutton.

Duberman, Martin, Vicinus, Martha, and Chauncey, George Jr. (1989). *Hidden from history: Reclaiming the gay and lesbian past.* New York: Penguin.

Dufty, William F. (1956). *Lady sings the blues: Billie Holiday.* New York: Doubleday & Co.

Edelman, Murray. (1994). The gay and lesbian vote and estimates of population size. New York: Voter News Service.

Equality Project (1993). Equality principles on sexual orientation. New York: Wall Street Project.

Faludi, Susan (1991). *Backlash: The undeclared war against American women.* New York: Crown.

Friskopp, Annette and Silverstein, Sharon (1994). *Straight jobs, gay lives.* New York: Simon and Schuster.

Gentry, Curt (1991). *J. Edgar Hoover: The man and his secrets.* New York: W.W. Norton.

Gilfoyle, Timothy J. (1992). *City of Eros: New York City, prostitution, and the commercialization of sex, 1790-1920.* New York: W.W. Norton.

Gore, Al (1992). *Earth in the balance: Ecology and the human spirit.* Boston: Houghton Mifflin.

Hammer, Michael and Champy, James (1993). *Reengineering the corporation.* New York: HarperBusiness.

Handlin, Oscar and Handlin, Mary E. (1975). *The wealth of the American people.* New York: McGraw-Hill.

Hofstadter, Miller and Hofstadter, Aaron (1972). *The United States.* New York: Prentice-Hall.

James, Burnett (1984). *Billie Holiday.* New York: Hippocrene Books.

Janus, Samuel S. (1994). *Janus report on sexual behavior.* New York: John Wiley.

Johnson, Otto, ed. (1994). *The 1994 Information Please Almanac.* Boston: Houghton Mifflin.

Katz, Jonathan (1976). *Gay American history: Lesbians and gay men in the U.S.A.* New York: Cromwell.

Katz, Jonathan (1995). *The invention of heterosexuality.* New York: Penguin.

Kaufman, Louis (1980). *Essentials of advertising.* San Diego: Harcourt Brace Jovanovich.

Kearney, Elizabeth I. and Bandley, Michael (1990). *Customers run your company: They pay the bills!* Provo, UT: Community Press.

Kearney, Elizabeth I. and Bandley, Michael J. (1990). *People power: Reading people for results.* Provo, UT: Community Press.

Larson, Erik (1992). *The naked consumer: How our private lives become public commodities.* New York: Henry Holt.

Lieb, Sandra R. (1981). *Mother of the blues, a study of Ma Rainey.* Amherst, MA: University of Massachusetts Press.

Life. Welch, Paul (1964, June 26). The gay world takes to the streets, p. 68.

Lukenbill, Grant (1995). *Untold millions: Positioning your business for the gay and lesbian consumer revolution.* New York: HarperCollins.

March, Dave and Plimpton, George (1991). *50 Ways to Fight Censorship.* New York: Duke and Duchess Ventures.

Mickens, Ed (1994). *The 100 best companies for gay men and lesbians.* New York: Pocket Books.

Mickens, Ed (1994, April 19). Waging war on Wall Street. *The Advocate,* p. 41.

Miller, Alice (1991). *Breaking down the wall of silence: The liberating experience of facing painful truth.* New York: Dutton.

The Nation (1978, April 15), p. 434.

National Opinion Research Center (1992). *The national health and social life survey.* Chicago: University of Chicago.

The New York Times (1994, September 6). Gay presence leads revival of declining neighborhoods.

The New York Times (1995, May 30), p. A5.

Newsweek (1994, February 14). Homophobia, politics and issues, p. 42.

Nussbaum, Bruce (1990). *Good intentions: How big business and the medical establishment are corrupting the fight against AIDS.* New York: Atlantic Monthly Press.

Oliver, Paul (1959). *Kings of Jazz: Bessie Smith.* New York: A. S. Barnes and Co.

Paglia, Camille (1992). *Sex, art, and American culture.* New York: Vintage.

Pomeroy, Wardell B. (1972). *Dr. Kinsey and the Institute for Sex Research.* New York: Harper & Row.

Popcorn, Faith (1991). *The Popcorn report.* New York: HarperCollins.

Population Council (1995, May 30). Families in focus.

Posener, Jill (1982). *Spray it loud.* Routledge and Kegan Paul.

Rampersad, Arnold (1986). *The life of Langston Hughes.* New York: Oxford University Press.

Rand Corporation (1992). *Sexual orientation and U.S. military personnel policy: Options and assessment.* National Defense Research Institute MR-343-OSD.

Rector, Frank (1981). *The Nazi extermination of homosexuals.* Briarcliff Manor, NY: Stein and Day.

Ricklefs, Roger (1995, May 1). Big business boosts efforts to win share of gay market. *The Wall Street Journal,* Enterprise section, p. 1.

Roberts, Loue Mary and Berger, Paul D. (1989). *Direct Marketing Management.* Englewood Cliffs, NJ: Prentice Hall.

Russo, Vito (1987). *The celluloid closet.* New York: HarperCollins.

Rutledge, Leigh W. (1992). *Gay decades.* New York: Dutton.

Rutten, Peter, Bayers, Albert F. III, and Maloni, Kelly (1994). *Net guide, your map to the services, information and entertainment on the electronic highway.* New York: Random House Electronic Publishing.

Sante, Luc (1991). *Low life.* New York: Vintage.

Shilts, Randy (1993). *Conduct unbecoming: Gays and lesbians in the U.S. military.* New York: St. Martin's Press.

Signorile, Michelangelo (1993). *Queer in America: Sex, the media, and the closets of power.* New York: Random House.

Strub, Sean, Baker, Dan, and Henning, Bill (1994). *Cracking the corporate closet.* New York: HarperBusiness.

Summers, Anthony (1993). *Official and confidential: The secret life of J. Edgar Hoover.* New York: Putnam.

Tannahill, Reay (1980). *Sex in history.* Briarcliff Manor, NY: Stein and Day.

Thompson, Mark (1994). *Gay soul: Interviews and photographs.* San Francisco: HarperSanFrancisco.

von Hoffman, Nicholas (1988). *Citizen Cohn: The life and times of Roy Cohn.* New York: Doubleday.

The Wall Street Journal (1975, May 13). Campaigns to sell to homosexual market are being launched by more big firms.

West, Cornel (1993). *Race matters.* Boston: Beacon.

Winfeld, Liz and Spielman, Sue (1994). *Straight talk about gays in the workplace.* New York: AMACOM.

Yankelovich MONITOR (1994). *Time*/CNN News poll. Yankelovich Partners.

Index

Page numbers followed by the letter "f" indicate figures; those followed by the letter "t" indicate tables.

Order Your Own Copy of
This Important Book for Your Personal Library!

UNTOLD MILLIONS
Secret Truths About Marketing to Gay and Lesbian Consumers

_____ in softbound at $29.95 (ISBN: 1-56023-948-4)

COST OF BOOKS	☐ **BILL ME LATER:** ($5 service charge will be added) (Bill-me option is good on US/Canada/Mexico orders only; not good to jobbers, wholesalers, or subscription agencies.)
OUTSIDE USA/CANADA/ MEXICO: ADD 20%	
POSTAGE & HANDLING (US: $3.00 for first book & $1.25 for each additional book) Outside US: $4.75 for first book & $1.75 for each additional book)	☐ Check here if billing address is different from shipping address and attach purchase order and billing address information.
SUBTOTAL _____	Signature _____
IN CANADA: ADD 7% GST _____	☐ **PAYMENT ENCLOSED: $** _____
STATE TAX _____ (NY, OH & MN residents, please add appropriate local sales tax)	☐ **PLEASE CHARGE TO MY CREDIT CARD.** ☐ Visa ☐ MasterCard ☐ AmEx ☐ Discover ☐ Diner's Club
FINAL TOTAL _____ (If paying in Canadian funds, convert using the current exchange rate. UNESCO coupons welcome.)	Account # _____ Exp. Date _____ Signature _____

Prices in US dollars and subject to change without notice.

NAME _____

INSTITUTION _____

ADDRESS _____

CITY _____

STATE/ZIP _____

COUNTRY _____ COUNTY (NY residents only) _____

TEL _____ FAX _____

E-MAIL _____

May we use your e-mail address for confirmations and other types of information? ☐ Yes ☐ No

Order From Your Local Bookstore or Directly From

The Haworth Press, Inc.
10 Alice Street, Binghamton, New York 13904-1580 • USA
TELEPHONE: 1-800-HAWORTH (1-800-429-6784) / Outside US/Canada: (607) 722-5857
FAX: 1-800-895-0582 / Outside US/Canada: (607) 772-6362
E-mail: getinfo@haworthpressinc.com

PLEASE PHOTOCOPY THIS FORM FOR YOUR PERSONAL USE.

BOF96